The Fivefold Framework
Empowered for Unity

TODD MOZINGO

ALL SCRIPTURE QUOTATIONS:

Scripture quotations taken from the New American Standard Bible (NASB), Copyright ©1960, 1962, 1963, 1968,1971, 1972, 1973,1975, 1977, 1995 by The Lockman Foundation. Used by permission. Lockman.org

THE HOLY BIBLE, NEW INTERNATIONAL VERSION®, NIV® Copyright © 1973, 1978, 1984, 2011 by Biblica, Inc.® Used by permission. All rights reserved worldwide.

COPYRIGHT ©2024 BY Todd Mozingo

All Rights Reserved. No Part of this publication may be reproduced without the written permission of Todd Mozingo.

Editors: Kate Wood, Paul Garner

Graphics: Mariah Camacho

TABLE OF CONTENTS

INTRODUCTION	5
RESURRECTING APOSTLES	9
RESURRECTING PROPHETS	41
RESURRECTING EVANGELISTS	67
RESURRECTING PASTORS	91
RESURRECTING TEACHERS	117
RESURRECTING UNITY	145
RESURRECTING GIFTS	163
ABOUT THE AUTHOR	191
OTHER BOOKS BY TODD MOZINGO	193

FIVEFOLD FRAMEWORK

INTRODUCTION

Routine. Routine. Routine. Doing the same thing over and over again becomes routine. And routine can be the roadblock to "amazing," "incredible," "extravagant" or even..."Biblical." What am I getting at? The church in the United States, to a large extent, has become routine.

You may not see it, but think about it — church after church after church has the exact same fixed pattern: A one-hour church service, with a good Kids' Ministry, good coffee, good worship music and a feel-good message for the week from a dynamic teacher. Routine.

In each of those churches there is a Senior Pastor, a Worship Leader and a Youth Minister, followed by a church secretary. All of these churches operate in the same way. The Senior Pastor is the driver, the organizer, the influencer, the teacher, the evangelist and the pastor. The Senior Pastor is expected to be all things to all people.

How many times have you heard, "Let's ask the Pastor;" "It's the Pastor's decision;" "What direction does the Pastor want to go?" "We need to be under submission to the Pastor;" "The Pastor is God's choice for our shepherd and we need to honor that"?

Now, at face value, I am not refuting any of those statements. I am simply saying that the "routine" pattern of churches

INTRODUCTION

today is one of having a Senior, or Lead, Pastor that is the leader of all the ministries of the church. He is responsible for everything that happens at the church. He teaches on Sundays and, possibly, a class during the week. He shares the gospel with the congregation. He is expected to know what is ahead for the church and to plan for it. He is expected to do the hospital visits, the weddings and the funerals; because, after all, he is the Pastor.

It's a heavy load and we all know pastors who are burned out and have given up. Unfortunately, this is routinely how things are set up for the typical church congregation.

I believe that the reason we have pastors who burn out is because we have set in place a routine of systems that may not be Biblical. We place all of the duties of ministry on one central leader. Then, we are astonished when that leader collapses under the load, or finds an inappropriate outlet for the stress.

If that happens, we often pile accusations on top of that, accusations that our pastor is failing to be the perfect pastor in every area. If a pastor is focused on growing the church, he is considered not a "people person," but just a businessman. If the pastor spends all his time with people, he is told he needs to spend more time in the Word of God. If the pastor begins to prophesy, he is told that he is on an ego trip. It's a balancing act to be all things to all people regardless of who God made you to be as an individual.

As a pastor myself, I cannot express the number of times people have come to me to tell me how things "should be done" in the church. They come and say things like, "At my last church..." "The Bible says..." "Don't you think Christians should...?" or, "Don't ask me, you're the pastor!"

Often pastors are told that they are not doing enough in this area or that area—whatever the "pet" area of the church is for the person giving the input. I call people with too much input "Rookie Experts." They are people who have never done the job, but know *exactly* how it should be done.

What is the problem here? We have set up a routine, fixed, standard organization to run a church with a single leader responsible to meet every need. Now, let me CLEARLY say, "Anything with more than one head is a monster!" Chaos erupts when we have multiple visions, multiple directions, multiple focuses and multiple personalities involved.

What is the solution? How do we have a singular direction and yet many in leadership? Well, the good news is that we get the answer to destroy this routine system from Jesus Christ Himself.

Clearly, Jesus knows the downfall of having everything be contingent on one person and the downfall of having a multi-headed monster in charge. In Scripture, Jesus left us a plan called "ministries;" specifically, five ministries that equip the body of Christ to the fullness of Christ's intentions. Listed together, these have come to be known as the "fivefold ministry," and it is described in the Book of Ephesians.

In *The Fivefold Framework*, I want to take you on a journey of the system that Jesus Christ put in place to affect the body of Christ so that it grows, follows and spreads its leadership. This framework ensures that any church can become a mature body of Christ.

If you are a Senior Pastor and are concerned with giving up the reigns of leadership, you will see that, done correctly, there will only be one head to every church body.

INTRODUCTION

If you, as a pastor, are exhausted, then maybe it's time to consider how Christ wanted the leadership of the church to be organized. This book will help you release the power of leadership in your church!

FIVEFOLD FRAMEWORK

RESURRECTING APOSTLES

At Revive Church, we believe in a fully active fivefold ministry. The term, "fivefold ministry," comes from the Apostle Paul's letter to the church in Ephesus, (Greece), which is known in the Bible as the Book of Ephesians. In this letter, Paul makes it clear that the Lord Jesus Christ "gave" certain ministries to the church for a specific purpose. We are going to dig into that: What are these ministries? What are they for? How do they work? What do they mean to us as believers?[1]

Let's go straight to Scripture, to the fourth chapter of Ephesians, starting at verse 11:

> "And He [Christ] gave some as apostles, and some as prophets, and some as evangelists, and some as pastors and teachers,…"

You'll notice five ministries were given to the church. We're going to cover these five ministries, what they are and how they affect the church. We'll eventually cover all five, but in this chapter, we're starting with the ministry of the apostle.[2]

---

[1] Based on the message, "Resurrecting Apostles," August 4, 2024. https://reviveusnow.com/watch

[2] The messages in this book do not refer to the "New Apostolic Reformation" (NAR).

To understand why we're talking about these five ministries, you have to keep reading the verses that follow. Here is why we have these five ministries:

> "...for the equipping of the saints for the work of service, to the building up of the body of Christ; until we all attain to the unity of faith, and of the knowledge of the Son of God, to a mature man, to the measure of the stature which belongs to the fullness of Christ."

Now, if that didn't scare you, it should.

> "As a result, we are no longer to be children, tossed here and there by the waves and carried about by every wind of doctrine, by the trickery of men, by craftiness in deceitful scheming; but speaking the truth in love, we are to grow up in all aspects into Him who is the head, even Christ, from whom the whole body, being fitted and held together by what every joint supplies, according to the proper working of each individual part, causes the growth of the body for the building up of itself in love."

How many of you felt like that was 73 things in a run-on sentence? That's how I feel when I read it—it's so much. I could probably spend six months just on that set of Scriptures and what it means, because there's so much in there.

That's the goal of what the church is supposed to achieve—the unity of faith and maturity in Christ. But guess what? Paul just said, "Christ gave you these five ministries to help you accomplish it."

FIVEFOLD FRAMEWORK

Could There Be Apostles Today?

Some would say, as we begin this conversation about apostles, "Oh, there are no apostles today. You can't have apostles today because there was criteria laid out, that apostles had to meet, that nobody can meet today. There's no such thing as an apostle today." Well, we're going to look at that in Scripture.

Let's start with that criteria and where it was laid out — in the Book of the Acts of the Apostles, chapter one. Here's what's happening: Christ has been crucified, Christ has risen from the grave and Christ has met with the disciples. He spent 40 days with those disciples "speaking of the things concerning the kingdom of God."[3] At the close of that time, Christ said, "Now, I want you to wait in Jerusalem until what the Father promised comes upon you," which was the baptism in the Holy Spirit. "And, by the way, I'm now going to ascend to heaven." So, He leaves.

So, the disciples are waiting in Jerusalem, and they realize, "Wait a minute, we lost a guy…" There was a guy named Judas, the "son of perdition,"[4] as the Bible calls him, who betrayed Christ for the purpose of the crucifixion. "He is no longer with us. In fact, he has killed himself. So now we have eleven of us instead of twelve. We need to replace Judas."

Amongst themselves, they come up with criteria for how to choose someone to replace Judas. Reading from Acts, chapter one, verses 21-25, they decide,

> "Therefore it is necessary **that of the men who**

---

[3] Acts 1:3

[4] John 17:12

have accompanied us all the time that the Lord Jesus went in and out among us, beginning with the baptism of John until the day He was taken up from us, one of these must become a witness with us of His resurrection." So they put forth two men, Joseph called Barsabbas (who was also called Justus), and Matthias. And they prayed and said, 'You, Lord, who know the hearts of all men, show which one of these two You have chosen to occupy this ministry and apostleship from which Judas turned aside to go to his own place.'"

Here is the criteria the eleven apostles set: "This is what we need for the replacement of Judas." They needed someone who had been with Jesus while He was on earth, from the point of His baptism by John the Baptist until His resurrection and ascension.

Who Can Meet Those Requirements?

There it is—that's how they decided to replace Judas as an apostle. Given that, nobody *today* can meet those requirements. None of us were with Jesus at His baptism by John. None of us were there when Jesus rose from the dead and then ascended into heaven. Therefore, none of us can be apostles today. We cannot have apostles today. Apostles cannot exist today because nobody can meet those requirements, right?

I've got a problem with that when I continue to read the Bible. There was a man clearly called out as an apostle who did not meet those criteria. His name is Paul. Paul is referred to as an apostle many times in Scripture,[5] yet he did not accompany Jesus while He was on this earth from His baptism to His resurrection and ascension.

Paul even makes the argument that he is an apostle in his letter to the Galatians, chapters one and two. He essentially says, "I received the gospel by the revelation of Jesus Christ, and I perform the duties and actions of an apostle."

Then, when he makes the argument for being an apostle in his first letter to the Corinthian church, chapter nine, and in his second letter to the Corinthians, chapter 12, verses 11-12, he says, "I do the things that apostles do. I operate in miracles, signs and wonders." Therefore, Paul calls himself an apostle, and the rest of the group calls him an apostle. But the truth is, he didn't meet the original requirements set by the disciples. There's a hole in that argument.

By the way, there's another guy in the Bible who did not meet these requirements and yet was still called an apostle — Barnabas. In Acts, chapter 14, verse 14, Barnabas is referred to as an apostle, but he was not part of the original twelve.

Oh, wait! There was another guy in Scripture who was also called an apostle, but he doesn't meet the requirements of the original twelve — his name was Silas.[6]

Could it be that what we read in Acts, chapter one, was that the apostles were looking to replace Judas with someone who had the same experiences they had, so they could feel good that all of them had learned together and were taught together, and could again form a team of twelve together?

---

[5] Acts 14:14, Romans 1:1, 1 Corinthians 1:1, 1 Corinthians 9:1

[6] Acts 15:1-34

Could it be that their criteria was never meant to say that from then on there could not be apostles? Could there be apostles today?

The Chronological Consideration

There are a couple of different arguments, besides this qualification consideration, that people make from Scripture. The first one is that people say, "No, you can't have apostles today because of First Corinthians, chapter 12, verses 27-28."

Before I read this Scripture, I want to give you some context. This Scripture is written to a church body—the church body in Corinth, Greece. It's a letter from Paul written to the Corinthian believers. We know the letter as a book of the Bible called "First Corinthians." In chapter 12 of First Corinthians, verses 27-28, Paul writes:

> "Now you are Christ's body, and individually members of it. And God has appointed in the church, first apostles, second prophets, third teachers, then miracles, then gifts of healings, helps, administrations, various kinds of tongues."

People will take this Scripture and argue, "See, there's the proof that God appointed apostles *first*, back in the first century, back at the beginning of the church, and those were the only apostles, because they were the ones appointed first. That tells us that the twelve apostles started the church..." As I'm listening to this argument, what goes through my head is, "That would mean that Christ gave us apostles first to start the church, but then after those twelve apostles, He would then give us prophets..."

Let me ask you something—in the New Testament, who are the prophets that came after the apostles? It says that was second: He gave "second prophets." And now, by the way, after those prophets, He gave teachers. Who are the teachers that came third?

In other words, if you're going to say that "first" means those twelve apostles present in Acts, chapter one, then we must say, "Next should be a group of prophets, because He gave the prophets second." But I don't see prophets listed out like I do the original twelve apostles.

By the way, if that were true, that God gave "first apostles, second prophets, third teachers, then miracles,..." chronologically, it would mean that miracles could not happen until after the prophets and the teachers were given, because they were "after" the prophets and the teachers. But, if I read my Bible correctly, it says the apostles were performing miracles. How could they perform miracles, if there had to be prophets and then teachers before there could be miracles?

Following that argument, there could also be no "gifts of healings, helps, administrations, various kinds of tongues" until *after* miracles were given. I don't see this process laid out chronologically like that in Scripture.

The Authority Consideration

So, if it's not a chronological discussion—first, second, third, and then, and then, and then—if that's not chronological, what could Paul have meant by "first," "second," "third," "and then..."?

I believe there are two other options to discuss to determine what he's trying to say. One option is, could it mean that Paul was actually laying out an authority structure? In other words, the apostles are to be first—they're on top; and then the prophets, well, they're second; they come after apostles in authority; and then the teachers would be third in line of authority; and then miracles would be next in line, and so on?

I'm not comfortable with that, however, because if you take the authority-sequence stance, it would mean that people who work in miracles are in higher authority than people who work in "helps," because miracles came *before* helps in the authority structure.

It would mean that teachers are of higher-ranking authority than those who would work in miracles or administration or who speak in tongues. So, those who are teachers are in authority over those who speak in tongues?

In other words, like the chronological consideration, if you're going to use the authority sequence, you would have to use it all the way through the list. You would have to say that the first group were in higher authority than the next, right down the line.

Then the question becomes, "Where in Scripture does it ever say a person who speaks in tongues is lower in authority than a prophet or a teacher?" I don't see the authority consideration coming up in Scripture. I don't believe Paul was talking about an authority-ranked structure. That doesn't make sense, because we don't see a level of authority given to different gifts anywhere else.

The Sequential Consideration

But here's what I think does make sense in this Scripture in First Corinthians: These are ministries, in a series, given to the church body at Corinth. Do you remember Paul started the conversation by saying, "You are Christ's body... and God gave first..."?

Paul is writing to the church in Corinth and saying, "You're a body of Christ. As an apostle, I came to Corinth and I started a church." The apostle came first. Paul had established the church of Corinth on a missionary journey. "Then there was a prophetic voice that came into play as you grew as a church." Could that be what Paul meant?

Maybe I can make this a little clearer by venturing to say that most of us have been to another church. Have you noticed that other churches have different focuses, different missions, different things they're going after? For example, some churches are all-in to feed the hungry in their territory. Some are all about missions; they send people around the world. Some are all about training; that's what they do. Every church body has a vision given to it by God.

When we started Revive Church, this is what the Lord said to me: "I want a church that puts the Word of God and the Spirit of God back together, and I want it to be a house where anyone can encounter God." That was the vision; that was the mission; that was a prophetic word we received for who we will be, for who we are, in Revive Church.

After that, there needed to be teachers next to grow the church. It doesn't take long to figure out, when you're talking about teachers, Paul may have been talking about the ministry of a teacher, or he may have been talking about those who teach. Evangelists teach, pastors teach, teachers teach.

The sequential consideration makes sense to me, especially when you put the First Corinthians list next to the list from Ephesians, chapter four. First, you have an apostle come and say, "We're going to start a church here." We get a prophetic word for what we're going to do with that congregation, and then the evangelists go out and lead people to Christ.

When they lead people to Christ, somebody's got to pastor those people; somebody's got to help them. Once we get them in a position where they feel good about being in this place, then we've got to have some teaching. We've got to disciple those people. We've got to raise them up, so the evangelists and pastors and teachers begin to work with the people.

Now go back to the First Corinthians list and notice the sequence: When you pastor people, when you teach people, what begins to happen through that discipleship? They begin to understand the giftings. They understand, "We can speak in tongues! Wow, healing is available today!" And so those things, later in the list, are the next obvious sequence of things to happen in that church.

The Fivefold Ministry in Order

Allow me to clarify what I'm saying. In Ephesians, chapter four, Paul says, "Here are the five ministries given to the church." In First Corinthians, he says, "There's a bit of an order as to how they are given in a church." Let's see how those go together.

Apostles come first. What do apostles do? I'll talk about it later, but they initiate, they lead, they develop, they start churches. Do you know what the word "apostle" actually means? The word "apostle" actually means "one sent forth with orders." So, by definition, they are the ones sent out with an order to do something.

Next, prophets give God's word for the church body or the territory. I'm absolutely fine with every church having a different function, a different mission, a different goal. Why?

Because we're all put into our territory to accomplish different things. We get our particular goals through prophets that God provides, through prophetic words.

Then, you have the evangelists, pastors and teachers. Evangelists work in miracles and gifts of healing, which were next in the First Corinthians passage. Pastors work in "helps" and administration, caring for people, which is next in the list in First Corinthians. Finally, teachers disciple people in doctrines, ministry and giftings. So, the sequential consideration begins to make sense as you look at the initiation of a church body.

Given this perspective, I hope we can agree that it is certainly possible to have apostles today. In fact, Paul is saying that God has given apostles to the church.

A Ministry, Not A Title

I'm finally getting to my subject for this chapter: Resurrecting Apostles. I think something has happened in the church with the term "apostles" that has messed us up as a church. I'm not talking about Revive Church; I'm talking about the church as a whole. In the kingdom of God, we have gotten messed up about apostles. Why? Because we've turned it into a title instead of a ministry.

Let me explain. If I were to ask you the question, "What is a teacher?" you would say, "Well, it's somebody that takes information that we don't understand and presents it to us in a way that makes sense, so we can learn from it. We gain knowledge because they teach us something." We don't say, "A teacher is a teacher;" we describe what a teacher does. "What does the teacher do?"

If you look at someone who is an evangelist, you might ask, "What is an evangelist?" Well, that's someone who shares the gospel. Their goal is to lead people to Christ. They often have the opportunity to work in miracles, signs and wonders as a confirmation of the Word. This is what they do.

In other words, when we look at the title of "teacher" or "evangelist," we don't think title; we think purpose: "What do they do? What is their ministry? What is their purpose?"

Let's apply that to the other names. What is a pastor? We won't go into detail here, but we've used this term "pastor" to describe a "shepherd" of believers, an overseer, someone who cares for people. We've given that title to whoever is running the church. That doesn't mean the person who's running your church *is* a pastor, because a pastor is one who cares for people. They have a divine endowment by God to especially want to reach out to people, to seek relationships, to make sure others are okay.

Next, what is a prophet? A prophet is someone who is getting a divine word to be delivered. That's just it in a basic nutshell. God says, "I'm going to use you to deliver these words. I want you to deliver them for Me." They could be words of encouragement or they could be prophetic words about the future.

So, what is an apostle? Is it a title within the church, or is an apostle someone "sent out" with a mission to build the kingdom of God? I believe that's it. Let's talk about what they *do*. We have to start looking at what they do, instead of looking at the title they were given.

The five things listed in Ephesians, chapter four, are ministries that Christ gave to the church. They are not titles and positions given to the church. Do you remember the passage in Acts, chapter one, when they were selecting a replacement for Judas? They said, "We need to select someone to occupy this ministry."

> "You, Lord, who know the hearts of all men, show which one of these two You have chosen **to occupy this ministry and apostleship..."**

Even they were saying, "This is a *ministry*. This is not a title. It's a ministry we want someone to function in." So they picked Matthias and said, "This is the guy to occupy this ministry."

In today's charismatic world—no offense—we get crazy on titles. We get a little weird sometimes. I'm not trying to offend anybody, but I know an individual who titles himself "Senior Chief Apostle." What is that? I'm wondering, "Who can give you that title? Who decides that you're not only an apostle but a Senior Apostle, and then of the Senior Apostles, you're the Chief?" It gets weird.

Never do any of the apostles identified in the New Testament announce themselves by the title of "Apostle." They may claim that they are apostles, but they don't step into a city and say, "I, Apostle John, have a word for you today..."

Do you know that there is only one place in the entire Scripture—66 books of the Bible—where "apostle" is used as a title? That is, capital "A," someone was identified with the title of "apostle"? It happens to be in the letter to the Hebrews, chapter three, verse one. This is what it says:

> "Therefore, holy brethren, partakers of a heavenly calling, **consider Jesus, the Apostle and High Priest of our confession;..."**

Jesus is the only One who took "apostle" as a title. No one on earth has "apostle" as a title. It's a ministry. And by the way, just so we can confirm, we talked about what the definition of "apostle" was—one who is sent out with orders. What did Jesus do? He was sent out from heaven to come to this earth with orders to redeem man back to God. He is THE Apostle. Hallelujah!

The Purpose of the Fivefold Ministry

So, Christ gave the church—hear me out, the new phrase we're going to be using—the "apostolic ministry." There is an apostolic ministry; there is a prophetic ministry; there is an evangelistic ministry; there is a pastoral ministry; there is a teaching ministry. What is the purpose for these ministries? Let's go back to Ephesians, chapter four, verses 11-13:

> "And He gave some as apostles, and some as prophets, and some as evangelists, and some as pastors and teachers, **for the equipping of the saints for the work of service, to the building up of the body of Christ**; until we all attain to the unity of faith, and of the knowledge of the Son of God, to a mature man, to the measure of the stature which belongs to the fullness of Christ. As a result, are no longer to be children,…"

Paul said, "Here are the ministries in the church and this is what the ministries will do: they will equip the saints." How? By giving you a title? No, by letting you operate in the ministry. "They're going to build up the body of Christ." How? By giving us all titles, so we feel built up? No, by allowing people to operate in their ministry until "we all attain to the unity of faith." How? Through the working of each ministry until we are mature and no longer children.

Is it, "I'm not a child anymore because now I have an adult title"? No. There are ministries that are building me up to make me mature, so that I can speak the truth in love, so that I can grow up — not so I can get a title — but so I can grow up and become mature "to the fullness of Christ."

Are They Still For Today?

So here's the million-dollar question: Do we still have apostles, prophets, evangelists, pastors and teachers today? I'm going to ask you another question, posed by this same Scripture: Do we have, in the church at large, even in this body, a unity of faith, the knowledge of the Son of God? Are we currently a "mature man, to the measure of the stature that belongs to the fullness of Christ"?

That's why I said earlier, this statement should scare you. I don't think I'm mature to the fullness of Jesus Christ. I've got a long way to go. I love the sanctification process, but I'm not there yet. Why am I bringing that out? Because if we do not have a "unity of faith, and of the knowledge of the Son of God, to a mature man, to the measure of the stature that belongs to the fullness of Christ," then we still need these ministries. That's why the ministries were given to us — so that we can attain maturity. But, we haven't attained it yet, so we must still need these ministries.

Secondly, let me ask you this question: When you've visited other churches, did those churches have teachers? Yes. Did those churches have pastors? Yes. Did those churches have evangelists? Yes. Well, if those other churches still have those three, why did they kick out the prophets and the apostles? Where do you read in Scripture that, "Christ gave you these five things, but eventually, you'll only need three of them. At some point, we'll get rid of these other two."?

Paul was telling the church at Corinth, after Christ is resurrected, after the work of the first twelve is already done,

"Christ is giving you the apostolic ministry." Nowhere does he say three of the five ministries will be good, but two of them will go away. I don't know why we've decided to kick two ministries out when Scripture doesn't tell us to kick those two out.

Some will say, "Well, here's the problem: We cannot meet the requirements of the apostle laid out in Acts,..." which, okay, I understand where you're coming from on that; I just don't think it's a valid argument. "And, by the way, we no longer need the prophets because we have the Holy Spirit in us. In the Old Testament, they didn't have the Holy Spirit in them. When the Holy Spirit came upon a prophet, the prophet would say what God had said to say. But now we have the Holy Spirit in us, so now we are the prophetic voice. We don't..." Okay, fine. You want to make that argument? That's why you don't need an apostle and that's why you don't need a prophet?

Let's go back to Scripture. Doesn't it say in the Gospel of John, chapter 14, and in John's first letter, chapter two, verse 27, that the Holy Spirit will teach us? Then why do we need teachers? We've got the Holy Spirit to teach us. He's going to teach me.

Doesn't Scripture say that Jesus is our Good Shepherd?[7] Therefore, He's our Pastor. Then why do I need a pastor? I've got a Good Shepherd in Jesus, so I don't need that position at all.

Doesn't Scripture say in John, chapter six, verse 44, that God will draw us to salvation, that His kindness leads us to repentance? I guess we don't need an evangelist then; God's

---

[7] John 10:11-18

going to do that. In fact, I don't need any part of this fivefold ministry anymore, because I've got the Holy Spirit, God and Jesus. We're done.

I'm hoping I make my point. Paul said Christ gave all five of these ministries to the church because we need them all until we are mature, and we're not mature yet.

The Apostolic Ministry

Let's talk about apostles. What is an apostle in the sense of the apostolic ministry? Are you, by chance, apostolic? Do you know if Christ gave this ministry to you for the building up and the maturing of the church? Are you operating in the ministry of the apostolic?

By definition, an apostle starts ministries. He is sent out with orders; he builds; he organizes; he administrates; he solves the ongoing problems. An apostle is looking to establish the kingdom of God on earth.

Apostles are Kingdom-growth leaders. They want systems; they want leaders; they want delegation put in place, for the maturing of the church. They are looking to develop and activate other people. They are catalysts for church-starts and on-going improvements. They settle doctrinal disputes.

They set gifts, ministries and people in motion for the future of the maturity of the church. Apostolic people are structurally- and organizationally-minded.

These Ministries Work Together

Yet, there are four other ministries. I want to contrast what it means to be apostolic, as opposed to what it means to operate in those four other ministries, when something happens in the life of someone in the church.

Let's say, for my example purposes today, that in your life, in your circle of family or friends or people you have around you, someone close to you dies. How do these ministries come into play for you? Where do we go from there?

When that happens, the pastors come to the forefront. They know you're hurting. They want to be there with you. They want to find out what your needs are. They want to minister to you, because they know you're in a place of confusion or hurt or loss. Everything in them says, "I need to know if you're okay." "How can I help you be okay through this tragedy?" That's a pastor.

What does an evangelist do? An evangelist wants to come and say, "Look, I know you just lost somebody, but do you know Jesus? Because, one day, this can happen to you and I don't want your friends to be sitting around wondering if you went to an eternity with God or not. I want to share the gospel with you."

What does the prophet do? Prophets, in general, are focused on, "Are we living a holy life?" "Are we listening to God?" "Are we repentant about our sin?" So, they may come to you and say, "Let's look at what we saw in this person's life. Were they walking in a holy way? What can we learn from them about you, so that you can walk in holiness?"

What does the teacher do? The teacher wants to come and explain to you what the Scriptures say about death. What happens? Where do we go from here? We've heard that "to be absent from here is to be present with the Lord."[8] What does that mean? What does the Bible say? How does that

---

[8] 2 Corinthians 5:6-8

transition work? What do we do? So, you have a teacher that's involved.

Now, let me tell you what the apostle does when someone close to you dies: the apostle wants to make sure you have someone to come and pastor you. The apostle wants to make sure that someone is there to share the gospel with your family. The apostle wants to make sure there's someone there to bring you a life lesson about living holy out of this. The apostle wants to make sure that someone is there to explain to you what that Scripture means when it says, "… and these people don't enter the kingdom of God and these people do…" and "What does that mean for my relative?" They're going to explain that; they're going to teach it.

The apostolic person *knows* they are not the best person to be there for you in that moment. They want to make sure you're okay and that someone is there to share the gospel with you and to find out if you're living a holy life and what you've learned from the experience and to explain what the Word of God says, but the apostle recognizes, "It's not me." He knows there are people that God has equipped to do those things, and he also knows it's not him. The apostle's job is to make sure those ministers are trained, equipped and available for people in crisis.

Apostolic people know that if there's not somebody available to meet your needs, then as apostolic people, we haven't done our job. In other words, as an apostolic person myself, I would realize, "I didn't set things in place for you. I don't have anybody to go care for you. I don't have anybody to teach you and to answer the questions that you're going to have. That was my job to set up the organization to make sure that you were taken care of."

The "Sent-Out" Ones

Let's go to Scripture and confirm some of the roles within an apostolic ministry. In other words, let's look at what the apostles did and then ask, "Does this connect with you? Would you be thinking that way? Would you do that kind of thing?"

There's actually a definition that Jesus gives in the Gospel of Mark, chapter three, verse 14, of what an apostle is. Here we have Jesus appointing the twelve disciples:

> And He appointed twelve, so that they would be with Him and **that He could send them out to preach, and to have authority to cast out demons.**

They have authority and they're sent out to preach. Some of you may be thinking, "Well, what's the difference between preaching and teaching? Is the apostle a teacher or is he a preacher?" Here Jesus said, "I sent them out to preach."

Teaching is when I'm exposing knowledge to you. I'm trying to get your understanding level up. I'm trying to let you see what that Scripture says, how it applies to your life, what to do with it. When I'm preaching, I'm trying to motivate you to do these things. I'm trying to get you to step forward and accept Christ. I'm trying to get you to step forward and start a Bible study at your workplace. I'm preaching to you. I'm trying to motivate you to do things.

Another function of an apostle is given in the Book of Acts, chapter 14, verse 23. Paul is an apostle. He's in a city called Derbe.

> **When they had appointed elders for them in every church,** having prayed with fasting, they commended them to the Lord in whom they had believed.

What did the apostles do? They said, "We've got to leave Corinth. We've got to leave Ephesus, but we can't leave the people without an overseer group. So we're going to appoint some overseers, or elders, to watch over this ministry while we're gone." They appoint elders.

In Jerusalem, Peter, the apostle, confirmed the Word of God. Acts, chapter two, verses 14-17 tells us,

> But Peter, taking his stand with the eleven, raised his voice and declared to them: "Men of Judea and all of you who live in Jerusalem, let this be known to you and give heed to my words. For these men are not drunk, as you suppose, for it is only the third hour of the day; but **this is what was spoken of through the prophet Joel**:…"

And he goes on to explain to them what was spoken through the prophet Joel. He's saying, "I'm confirming for you today that Joel said there would be a day when God would pour out His Spirit on all mankind."

> "…'AND YOUR SONS AND YOUR DAUGHTERS SHALL PROPHESY,
> AND YOUR YOUNG MEN SHALL SEE VISIONS,
> AND YOUR OLD MEN SHALL DREAM DREAMS;…'"

He's confirming that that day is now; that's the day. He's confirming for them what the Bible says.

Apostles settle doctrinal decisions, as in Acts, chapter 15. For background, the disciples all know that Jesus was sent for the Jewish nation, as their Messiah. But then, all of a sudden, Peter goes to meet with Cornelius, a Roman centurion. Cornelius is not Jewish; he's a Gentile. Cornelius and his household all get saved and they start speaking in tongues.[9] And it's like, "Wait a minute, wait a minute, wait a minute!"

Now the Gentiles get to come to know Christ as Savior! "What are we going to do about that?" Peter and the others go back to Jerusalem and meet with James, the brother of Jesus, who happens to be an apostle. They say, "How do we handle this? This is new. What do we do with it?" This is what James says, from Acts, chapter 15, verses 19-21:

> **"Therefore it is my judgment that we do not trouble those who are turning to God from among the Gentiles**, but that we write them that they abstain from things contaminated by idols and from fornication and from what is strangled and from blood. For Moses from ancient generations has in every city those who preach him, since he is read in the synagogues every Sabbath."

What did he just say? He said, "Here are some of the things that Gentiles are doing. We need to tell them to stop doing those things if they receive Christ as their Savior. But, they should begin going to the synagogues, because in the synagogues they're going to be taught." James is making decisions on what to do in the church.

Paul, the apostle, mentored Timothy. Look at this mentoring statement in Paul's second letter to Timothy, chapter one, verses six through seven:

> "For this reason I remind you to kindle afresh the gift of God which is in you through the laying on of my hands...."

---

[9] Acts 10:23-48

Paul is writing this in a letter; he's not there. He's saying, "I was with you. I prayed for you with the laying on of my hands. There was a gift placed in you, and now I want you to kindle that afresh."

> "...For God has not given us a spirit of timidity, but of power and love and discipline."

He's saying, "Timothy, come on, man! I have poured into you. Let that rise up in you. Don't be timid, be strong, be powerful! Operate in love, with a sound mind." Paul is mentoring him.

If you go on to read about Peter and Paul, they started churches in Antioch, Ephesus, Smyrna, Pergamon, Thyatira, Sardis, Philadelphia, Laodicea, Colossae and Hierapolis.[10] If you look at James and Thomas and Matthew, who are apostles, they were starting in different countries of the world, in Indonesia and places that you probably don't even hear about, but it's recorded in history.

You have apostles like John and Matthew who wrote gospels of doctrine for us to understand. The apostolic ministry represents the initiators and mentors given to the church to assist growth, organization and development of the church into a place of maturity.

Is This You?

Let me let you into the mind of how an apostolic person thinks. If I go through this and you say, "Man, that's me. You think like me," or you say, "I don't think like that," that's

---

[10] Acts 11:26; Revelation 1:11; Colossians 1:2, 4:13

okay, because you do think like one of the other ministries and we'll get to that in the coming chapters.

A person in the apostolic ministry thinks like this:
- What needs to be put in place to develop the people?
- How are they going to learn?
- How are they going to grow?
- Are we covering all the bases we need to, for this season, in this territory?
- Are we who we are supposed to be to this territory?
- Do we have people to train, and do I have people trained up to train people?
- Where will we be as a church two years from now?
- Where will we be five years from now?
- Where will we be ten years from now?
- What do we need, in the way of resources, to fulfill the plans that God has given us?
- How do we organize this thing for the best results?

Underlying all these questions, you must realize, most apostolic people are not relationally-based. They are goal- and vision-based. "Where are we going? My job is to help set us up to get there." That type of thinking is very natural; it's secondhand for the apostle.

A Personal Example

I'll give you a quick personal story: I didn't go into ministry until I was 40 years old. Before I was in ministry, I was in manufacturing, the director of operations, a plant manager; I made product. In the business world, the "headhunters" — the people who help you get jobs — they knew me as a "turnaround guy." What's a turnaround guy? When a company is struggling, when they're not making enough money, when they're not getting enough product out of the door, you hire Todd Mozingo. Why? Because he comes in and he can just *see* what's wrong. He can see, "This is laid out wrong." He can see you're getting your product wrong. He can see your quality levels are killing you.

So, for me, I could go in and it was just easy. I could walk into an interview and a guy would take me out to the manufacturing plant and say, "This is not working like it should. What's wrong?" It wouldn't take me very long at all to say, "Well, that's organized wrong. You're doing a repetitive thing and you're not set up for a repetitive function. You need Kanban bins so your materials get to your floor quicker." It was easy for me.

What I'm saying is that apostolic ministry was given to me before I was brought into the Kingdom. Manufacturing was my training and my practice ground, so that when God brought me into the Kingdom, those things that were natural to me could be used in the Kingdom.

Training Required

If this is the way you think, then maybe you should be exploring in prayer before God, "Why? Why did you give me this ministry? Why do I think this way?" But, figuring out that you operate in the apostolic ministry does not mean you are ready to lead. There is training. When God told me I was going into ministry, it was three years later before I actually went into ministry.

There are times when you need to be under other apostolic leaders, where you need to understand the church, where you need to understand your own flaws or your lack of need for the other ministries. Those things have got to be brought to your attention. Let me tell you the number one best training ground for the apostle. If you are apostolic, this will be your number one best training: failure.

Failure will teach you more than anything, if you're apostolic, because it'll hit you like a ton of bricks. You'll think, "What in the world did I do wrong?" "I will not do *that* again!" "I need to rearrange and do some things differently, because I don't like that feeling." Many people that think they're apostolic are actually not. It's okay. Give me five more chapters and you'll be okay with that statement.

How do you know if you're actually apostolic? There is one measurement in the Bible that applies to all ministries and all giftings. If you want to know if you operate in a certain gifting or ministry, you need to look at the fruit. Is there fruit that you are apostolic? What would be the fruit? Is what you build substantial? Is it sustaining? Is it growing? Is it organized? Does it have structure? Is it succeeding?

Some people think they're apostolic, but they're not. This is where things like inner healing and "Narrow Gate 2 Narrow Path" come into play.[11] Why do I say that? Because, oftentimes, the people who think they're apostolic are just people who need control. They need a title, they need authority. They don't really know how to grow a thing, but they want to be put in charge of it. That points to a need inside, that they're trying to meet, because they don't know they're operating out of that need, instead of out of a call to the apostolic ministry.

---

[11] https://reviveusnow.com/ministries/healing /
https://www.narrowgate2narrowpath.com/

Things to Watch Out For

What's the downside if you're apostolic? If that's the ministry that God has given to you, what are the traps? What do you have to watch for?

- You've got to make sure you don't turn your calling into a dictatorship.
- You've got to make sure that you're not doing it out of a love of being in charge.
- You've got to watch things like pride.

Why? Because when you succeed you want to take the credit. But, if you're succeeding, you wouldn't be succeeding because of you. You're succeeding because of what God gave you to do. We must constantly recognize that, without Him, we cannot succeed.

- You have to watch your attitude.
- You have to watch the abuse of leadership.
- You have to watch this, "God called me to lead, so y'all should follow me!" attitude.

Listen, if you're not producing fruit in your ministry, why would anybody follow you?

There's a lack of humility that can come in the apostolic ministry, but the true apostolic ministry feels a responsibility to steward, not only the ministry gift they were given, but the church. A church rises and falls based on apostolic leadership.

So, an apostle has to constantly look at himself and ask, "Am I doing what You asked me to do, God?" "Am I using the gifting that You've given me in order for this church to move forward?" Or, "Am I a hindrance in some way to what's going on?"

Apostles Needed

The church needs apostolic people. As a congregation, and as the church as a whole, in the nation and in the world, we need apostolic people. They are organizationally-minded. They are growth-minded.

We need apostolic people who are humble, who recognize, "This is a gift and I'm meant to steward this gift and I could mess it up." We need apostolic people who care about the kingdom of God. "What are we doing in this territory?" "What are we doing in this nation?" "Is the church going to rise up in our government, or are we just going to continue to hand it over to the enemy?"

The church needs apostolic people who know they need the other four ministries. You've got to know when you're not the best person to meet a need. You've got to know that there are people who are better at pastoring, people who know how to touch others' hearts, who know how to give them love.

Apostles have got to know that there are prophetic people who are hearing clearly from God and who can strengthen them, if they weren't so conceited that they won't listen to them.

Apostles have got to know that there are teachers, people who can roll out Scripture and doctrine to the body of Christ, so that others say, "Wow, I never even saw that…!"

Apostles have got to know that there are evangelists. For myself, I can share the gospel—I've shared the gospel many times. I've seen many people come to Christ, but I'm sharing a "teacher's gospel." What do I mean by that? When I share the gospel, I'm explaining what the Bible says about you and salvation. When you meet a true evangelist, they don't need Scripture in that heavy of a form. They tell you, "God loves you," and when you're hurting, they say, "God wants to come and rescue you right now, right in this moment." They ask, "Would you be open to what He has for you?" (By the way, I did not just say that evangelists don't use Scripture.)

Finally, I believe the church needs apostolic people who realize that there is a time of training to fully operate in the apostolic ministry. It's not a gift of "know all, be all, do all." It is a gift that is developed. It's a ministry that is developed and the church needs apostolic people who want to be trained.

One of the shortcomings of an apostolic person is, "Well, if God gave me this gift, then I should know what I'm doing. So let me just get in and do it." Then you find out that your arrogance and your pride just got in the way of the ministry He gave you.

God provides mentors, just as Paul was given to Timothy to raise Timothy up, so that Paul could leave and Timothy could do it on his own. There was a time of training.

Our Purpose

What are we doing in this set of messages? We are looking at why the Lord gave these five ministries to the church. What was His purpose? What was His goal? Paul states it very succinctly and clearly: it was to grow us up until we have unity in the faith, to make us mature, so that we can attain the fullness of Christ.

If we don't have five ministries operating fully, then we don't know unity and maturity and the fullness of Christ. We know part of it. We know some of it. But, we don't fully grow. We've got to identify who's operating in each ministry so that we can become mature and complete as a body.

If what I have explained about the apostolic ministry speaks to your heart, as in, "He's talking my game; He's describing me." "This is how I think." "I'm tired of everybody else telling me that I'm not personable enough or that I don't care enough, because this is the way I think." If you think and operate apostolically, instead of pastorally, it doesn't make you bad or wrong. It means that you are operating in a different ministry.

If you are apostolic, we need to know who you are. We need to start talking and developing plans of where we're going and what can work in this territory and how we can grow up and how we can organize for success.

Maybe you're pastoral? Maybe you're evangelistic? Maybe you're prophetic? Maybe you're a teacher? Guess what? We need you every bit as much as the apostle. Apostles can't start a thing without the other four ministries. They've got to be together, so that we're whole and complete.

If you believe you may be apostolic, please find a trusted prayer partner to confirm God's call for you. It won't be an impartation for the ministry — you believe you've already got that. We ask that you pray for God to speak to you clearly, that He would knock things like pride out of the way and would allow you to see what He really has planned for you. We are looking for those people who can begin searching with God, "Did You make me apostolic for Kingdom purposes?" "Is this the place where I can be trained to operate in the apostolic ministry?"

Father God, in the name of Jesus, we're here because You wanted us here. You picked us, at this time, in this territory, to be the body of Christ. Therefore, You have equipped us with these

FIVEFOLD FRAMEWORK

ministries and giftings, in order to operate in the fullness of what You have for us. Open our eyes to who You made us to be, so we can operate fully and maturely in this territory.
We love You and we thank You.
In Jesus' name, Amen.

RESURRECTING APOSTLES

RESURRECTING PROPHETS

Here at Revive Church, we understand that Christ gave ministries to His body, and we believe those ministries should be active and valid for today. In the last chapter, we provided Biblical support for our belief as to why an apostle or a prophet or an evangelist or a pastor or a teacher represents an active ministry today.[12]

Our baseline Scripture for this study comes from Paul's letter to the Ephesians, chapter four, verses 11-13.

> **"And He [Jesus] gave some as apostles, and some as prophets, and some as evangelists, and some as pastors and teachers,** for the equipping of the saints for the work of service, to the building up of the body of Christ; until we all attain to the unity of the faith, and of the knowledge of the Son of God, to a mature man, to the measure of the stature which belongs to the fullness of Christ."

From this, we see that Christ gave ministries to the church to equip it, to build it up, to fully accomplish what He wanted to accomplish. Again, if you want to know our reasoning for how these ministries are still active today, please review the

---

[12] Based on the message, "Resurrecting Prophets," August 11, 2024. https://reviveusnow.com/watch

last chapter, "Resurrecting Apostles." In this chapter, we're going to cover the ministry of the prophetic—the ministry of the prophet.

In the fall of 2023, we had Mr. Joseph Z, who I believe to be a prophetic voice in the church at large, come to this church. He spoke some things that I have seen to be accurate, including some things he spoke directly to me, in front of many. One of the things he said to me specifically was, "You have an apostolic mandate to wrangle prophets."

He also said, "The prophetic movement is like a drunken uncle, and we need to have the apostles come in and grab the wheel." Now, if you operate in the prophetic, let me say upfront, *I* didn't say that—one of your prophetic people said it.

Three Kinds of Prophecy

What we want to do here is dig into this role of the ministry of the prophet. I'll say from the beginning, I'm not interested in controversy. I'm not interested in having any kind of contention with those who operate in the prophetic. I do believe, however, that we're living in a time where there is a lot of false prophecy.

First of all, prophecy, as a whole, is kind of an intimidating subject to teach on. Why is that? I believe it's because there is a lot about it in Scripture, and there are misunderstandings about it that can bring division.

When we talk about the prophetic ministry, what exactly are we talking about? I think there are three kinds of prophecy laid out in Scripture. The first one is a prophetic voice that we have where we speak and encourage others. It's usually referred to simply as "prophesying." Paul said in his first letter to the Corinthians, "I wish that you all would prophesy."[13]

The second category is mentioned in Scripture as the "gift of prophecy."[14] I believe the gift of prophecy is a transmission of information for individual impact. We'll discuss that further on in the chapter.

Then, the third type of prophecy is the ministry of the prophetic that Christ gave to the church, which is indicated in this passage from Ephesians. That's what we're discussing here, mainly so that you can understand, if the way you think, the way you approach Scripture, and the way you approach ministry all seem to be in alignment with the prophetic, you can begin exploring how you were designed.

That You May Prophesy

So let's talk about, first of all, prophecy that we all do. In First Corinthians, chapter 14, verses one through four, Paul writes,

> "Pursue love, yet desire earnestly spiritual gifts, **but especially that you may prophesy**. For one who speaks in a tongue does not speak to men but to God; for no one understands, but in his spirit he speaks mysteries...."

Now, I'm not going to go into detail, but in a very simple statement, what Paul just said was, "When people are speaking in tongues, others don't know what they're saying. They're speaking in mysteries. They're speaking to God, and

---

[13] 1 Corinthians 14:5

[14] 1 Corinthians 12:4-11

we don't know what they're saying." But that's not true of prophesying. Paul continues,

> "...**But one who prophesies speaks to men for edification and exhortation and consolation.** One who speaks in a tongue edifies himself; but one who prophesies edifies the church."

We are called to edify one another. We are called to exhort one another. We are called to console one another. Now, outside of the conversation of the prophetic, Paul also wrote, in his first letter to the Thessalonians, chapter five, verse 11,

> "Therefore **encourage one another and build up one another**, just as you also are doing."

That word "encourage" means to exhort one another and build one another up. The word "edify" means to build up. Paul urges us to exhort one another, to edify one another, to encourage one another and to build one another up, "just as you are doing."

We see, then, that we don't have to have the gift of prophecy, or work in the ministry of the prophetic, to encourage other people. We're called to do that. It's important. It's critical to our growth. It's critical to our bonding.

It's just like, you don't have to have a gift or a ministry to pray for someone to be healed. We can all do that. You don't have to have a gift or a ministry to grow in the knowledge of the Word. You don't have to have a gift or a ministry to expect the miraculous, when you're in Christ. These are things we're all called to do as believers.

So, "prophesying," in this sense of the word, is something everyone in the church does. You can prophesy; it's called edifying, exhorting and encouraging the people around you. You often hear demonstrations of that from our times of

"Speaking Life" to each other. We're building other people up, encouraging them, prophesying.

The Gift of Prophecy

But there are also times when the Holy Spirit gives something called the "gift of prophecy." This is when the Holy Spirit gives "a word" — specific information — to someone about someone else and says, "I need you to speak that to this individual. You need to speak that into him or her. I've given you a gift — this word — that you will then speak into somebody else."

Let's discuss the gift of prophecy by looking at First Corinthians, chapter 12, verses four through ten. Paul writes,

> "Now there are varieties of gifts, but the same Spirit. And there are varieties of ministries, and the same Lord. There are varieties of effects, but the same God who works all things in all persons. **But to each one is given a manifestation of the Spirit for the common good....**"

This is why you have a spiritual gift — for the common good of the body. It's not so that you can have a podcast or so that you can be famous or popular; it's so that the common good of the church is ministered to.

> "...For to one is given the word of wisdom [that's a gift] through the Spirit, and to another the word of knowledge [that's a gift] according to the same Spirit; to another faith [that's a gift. We're not talking about the faith of salvation; we're talking about the gift of faith] by the same Spirit, and to another gifts of healing by the one

> Spirit, and to another the effecting of miracles, **and to another prophecy** [the gift of prophecy], and to another the distinguishing of spirits, to another various kinds of tongues, and to another the interpretation of tongues."

We call this the listing of the spiritual gifts that we have, and we see that there is a gift of prophecy. In simple terms, I believe the gift of prophecy is when the Holy Spirit tells you, "I need you to go talk to this person, and I need you to say this to that person. I'm giving you a prophetic word for them."

Now, just because God speaks to you does not mean you are a prophet. It also does not mean you're operating in the gift of prophecy. It's a gift given by the Holy Spirit to some, to be used to build up the common good of the church.

Furthermore, Paul goes on to say how important it is to exercise each of these gifts from a heart of love. In chapter 13 of First Corinthians, verses one through three, he says,

> "If I speak with the tongues of men and of angels, but do not have love, I have become a noisy gong or a clanging cymbal. **If I have the gift of prophecy**, and know all mysteries and all knowledge; and if I have all faith, so as to remove mountains, **but do not have love, I am nothing.** And if I give all my possessions to feed the poor, and if I surrender my body to be burned, but do not have love, it profits me nothing."

Paul clearly says there is a gift of prophecy. He also says that if I have it, but I demonstrate it without love, then don't listen to me—I am nothing.

The Ministry of the Prophet

So, we have prophesying that we all do. And, we have a gift of prophecy, which I believe is a gift used more one-on-one, under direction of the Holy Spirit in the moment. Then, thirdly, there is the ministry of the prophet. That's what we want to focus on here. For those of you who are not even aware yet that you operate in the ministry of the prophetic, what I want to do is stir it up in you, to see if that's the way God designed you.

I believe the ministry of the prophet is the one that scares most people in the church because we don't clearly understand it. In the Old Testament, there were people appointed by God to be prophets, people like Isaiah and Jeremiah and Hosea—we call them "prophets." There are books of the Bible written about those prophets and the messages they gave. They delivered words to the Israelite leaders of the day or to the children of God as a whole.

Sometimes the prophets told them what was coming ahead of them. Sometimes they said, "If we don't repent, these will be our consequences." Sometimes they went to the leaders and said, "This is what God wants you to do in this battle."

Often, we think of these prophets as, "Oh, they're the ones that are crying out in the wilderness, 'repent, for the day of the Lord is at hand.'" And so we tend to give them this ethereal spookiness. But, God used these prophets in the Old Testament to speak into leaders, to warn leaders, to actually appoint and anoint future leaders.

These prophets proclaimed the message of God to change the direction of a nation. They were attested and anointed by God to be messengers. If you just look up the word "prophet," it means "a messenger, a speaker for God." We know those guys from the Old Testament, but are there prophets today in the New Testament Church?

Are There Prophets Today?

In the passage we read from Ephesians, chapter four, verse 10, Paul says Jesus gave some as prophets to the church for the building up of the church until we attain to the "unity of the faith." And, we talked in the last chapter about how Christians today haven't yet accomplished this goal of unity, so these ministries must still be active.

Also, we talked about how the role of a prophet is a ministry; it's not a title. It is a designation that Christ has placed on some. Some of you are prophetic; some of you are prophets. That means that there is a ministry that you're operating in for the church. It's not a stamp of approval or a title that's put on you.

Scripture is clear that Christ has appointed prophets in the church today. What is the purpose of the prophetic ministry in the New Testament Church? I don't actually think it's different from the mission of the prophet in the Old Testament: to speak into the church body as a whole, to speak into the leaders, to help with identifying future leaders.

Does that mean that the only way that we can hear from God is through a prophet? No. I'm going to give you Scripture to clarify that you can hear from God without a prophet telling you what God is saying.

"I Will Pour Out My Spirit"

Let's go to the Gospel of John, chapter 16, verses 12-14. Jesus is speaking to His disciples on the night before His betrayal.

He tells them,

> *"I have many more things to say to you, but you cannot bear them now. But when He,* [the Holy Spirit], *the Spirit of truth, comes,* **He will guide you into all the truth;** *for He will not speak on His own initiative, but whatever He hears,* **He will speak; and He will disclose to you what is to come.** *He will glorify Me, for He will take of Mine and will disclose it to you. All things that the Father has are Mine; therefore I said that He takes of Mine and will disclose it to you."*

Understanding this passage brought a major change in my life, since I grew up thinking that everything is "Jesus, Jesus, Jesus." And it is! Jesus is my King; He is my Redeemer; He paid the price for me; He is my Savior. "Every knee will bow and every tongue will confess that Jesus Christ is Lord, to the glory of God the Father!" (Phil 2:10-11) Unequivocally, without doubt, Jesus is all of those things. But that same Jesus said, "I'm going to sit back at the throne, and you will be led by the Holy Spirit."

Now, I don't know how I can be led by the Holy Spirit if I can't hear the Holy Spirit, if the Holy Spirit isn't telling me what God is saying. Paul explains in his letter to the Romans, chapter eight, verses nine through eleven:

> "However, you are not in the flesh but in the Spirit [capital "S" — the Holy Spirit], if indeed the Spirit of God dwells in you. But if anyone does not have the Spirit of Christ, he does not belong to Him. If Christ is in you, though the body is dead because of sin, yet the spirit is alive because of righteousness...."

Notice the small "s" — he's talking about how your spirit is now brought to life because the Holy Spirit dwells in you.

> "...But if the Spirit of Him who raised Jesus from the dead dwells in you, He who raised Christ Jesus from the dead will also give life to your mortal bodies through His Spirit who dwells in you."

If you are in Christ, the Holy Spirit dwells in you. Jesus said He, the Holy Spirit, will guide you into all the truth, so the Holy Spirit will talk to you directly.

Paul writes about this further in First Corinthians, chapter two, verse nine:

> "...but just as it is written,
>
> 'THINGS WHICH EYE HAS NOT SEEN AND EAR HAS NOT HEARD, AND WHICH HAVE NOT ENTERED THE HEART OF MAN, ALL THAT GOD HAS PREPARED FOR THOSE WHO LOVE HIM.'
>
> For to us God revealed them through the Spirit; for the Spirit searches all things, even the depths of God."

What is this saying? We can hear from God, not through our ears, not through our eyes. He speaks to us through the Spirit. Clearly, emphatically, without question — you can hear directly from God through the Spirit who is alive in you.

A Note of Caution

Now, it can become confusing if you begin to think, "God spoke to me. Hey, I must be a prophet!" or "I must be working in the gift of prophecy." Not exactly — God can speak to you at any time and at any moment. Remember, God speaking to you doesn't give you a title; it's just God speaking to you.

If you've been in church very long, you begin to recognize that there are people who hear something from God and believe it's now their prophetic ministry to share that with others. They may come to your prayer meetings or call you up or meet you at church and say, "Do you know what God told me this week? He told me that you should be doing this and this." Let me tell you, it's possible that God never said to give that word to someone else. He was talking to you, and you got all up in the flesh thinking you had a word from God that you needed to deliver, but did you? If God was speaking to you, it's best to keep it to yourself and pray through it until He tells you to give it to someone else.

You may ask, "How do I know, then, if I'm operating in the prophetic ministry that Christ gave to the church?" Here's how you can know: Did Christ appoint you to be a prophet in the church today? If Christ appointed you to that ministry, then you have a ministry to operate in.

New Testament Examples

I believe the prophetic ministry today operates at the leadership and church level. Why? Because the gift of prophecy and prophesying to one another are there for the common good of the church body, but Christ appoints prophets to give direction to His people, to speak to His leaders, to work with where the church is going.

Let me give you some examples of what New Testament prophets said and did, so you'll see what I'm saying. In the Book of the Acts of the Apostles, chapter 11, verses 27-30:

> "Now at this time, some prophets came down from Jerusalem to Antioch. One of them named Agabus stood up and **began to indicate by the Spirit that there would certainly be a great famine all over the world.** And this took place in the reign of Claudius. And in the proportion that any of the disciples had means, each of them determined to send a contribution for the relief of the brethren living in Judea. And this they did sending it in charge of Barnabas and Saul to the elders."

Here, in the New Testament, a prophet said there would be a great famine coming to the world. He told the leadership of the church in Antioch and they were able to prepare. The text says that that famine did take place in the reign of the Roman Caesar, Claudius.

Another example of the ministry of the prophet is from Acts, chapter 13, verses one through three:

> Now there were at Antioch, in the church that was there, prophets and teachers: Barnabas, and Simeon who was called Niger, and Lucius of Cyrene, and Manaen who had been brought up with Herod the Tetrarch, and Saul. While they were ministering to the Lord and fasting, **the Holy Spirit said, "Set apart for Me Barnabas and Saul** [later known as Paul] **for the work for which I have called them."** Then, when they had fasted and prayed and laid hands on them, they sent them away.

What did we just see happen? The prophets that were in Antioch heard from the Spirit that the church needed to send out Barnabas and Saul. They declared that in that church, so the leadership laid hands on those two and sent them out.

Finally, in Acts, chapter 15, verse 32:

> Judas and Silas, also being prophets themselves, **encouraged and strengthened the brethren with a lengthy message**."

What are we saying here? We're saying that sometimes prophets talk too much! Judas and Silas had a "lengthy message" for the brethren who were there.

The New Testament prophetic voice—the prophetic ministry—gives direction for the people of God to the church as a whole, to the leaders in the church or to the church body to which they are assigned and, occasionally, to individuals. Their purpose is to relay information from God to certain people.

For The Building Up of the Church

Sometimes the information prophets give is for course-correction of the particular leadership of a particular church. In that sense, their role is very similar to the role of the Old Testament prophet.

Today, prophets speak to leaders and often speak to nations. They give directional assistance to the apostolic ministry. The apostolic ministry needs the prophetic ministry. Apostles need to get direction and course-correction from prophets. Apostles do not "report" to prophets and prophets do not "report" to apostles. These are co-ministries for the common good of the body. I believe the prophetic ministry's main work is to the church body and to the leadership and to the apostolic leaders.

In the charismatic church, one of the things that we have unintentionally done is we've taken people who operate in a prophetic ministry and we've made superstars out of them. "Oh, they're the most important!" "We need a podcast from them." "We need them to come to our church. If the prophet's in town, everybody's going to show up to see if they can get a word from the prophet."

We think that if we're struggling, we need to find somebody who's prophetic, so they can give us a word from God about what to do. Unfortunately, if you're at a service or a conference and someone who says they are prophetic says something to you, then you're likely to believe that it's set in stone and unquestionable.

But, look at what Paul says in First Corinthians, chapter 14, verses 29-33:

> **"Let two or three prophets speak, and let the others pass judgment**. But if a revelation is made to another who is seated, the first one must keep silent. For you can all prophesy one by one, so that all may learn and all may be exhorted; and **the spirits of prophets are subject to prophets;** for God is not a God of confusion but of peace, as in all the churches of the saints."

What did that just say? The phrase we use today is "prophets measure prophets." In other words, when somebody speaks prophetically, we have someone else whom we *know* operates in the prophetic ministry judge if it was a true prophetic word. Prophets measure prophets. When someone speaks, someone else we know, who operates in the prophetic, can say, "Yes, that was a prophetic word from the Lord."

Let The Others Judge

It sometimes happens that someone has come to me right before a service and has said, "Hey, I'm new here today, and I am a prophet. I have a word for your church." Here's my answer: "No, you don't. But, if you want to give it to our prophetic team, and if they tell me it's for our church, then we'll receive it." This is how we let prophets measure other prophets.

If someone, unknown to this body, comes in with a word for us, I'd be thinking, "I don't know who you are. I don't know what makes you a prophet. Was that self-titled? Do you just have a beef with the church and you want to give it? I don't know..." As a leader, I need the prophets of this body to measure any prophesies from outside prophets.

But, as a matter of fact, if you are a member of this body — for those of you who work in either a gift of prophecy or work in the prophetic ministry — if you get a word in the church service, and you feel like what the Lord is saying needs to be released in this house, this is what we ask you to do: go tell Kimo and Nathalie Bethea. They're going to measure or judge that word and either say, "Yes, that's a word for today," or "No, it's not."

I love you prophetic people, but it's possible to get confused with what is a personal prophetic word and what is a prophetic word for the church or for someone else.

Sometimes we think, "The Lord has told me this. I think the world needs to hear it!" Well, maybe. But first consider, if the Lord told *you*, then likely, *you* need to hear it. After you've considered the word, you can ask the Lord if you are to share it. If so, you can submit it to the prophetic ministry of this body. Make sense? I'm not being mean — I'm just saying that this is an easy place to get into the flesh.

Beware of False Prophets

Do you know that in the New Testament, it's called out eleven times to watch for false prophets? One example is from the Apostle John's first letter, chapter four, verse one. He says,

> "Beloved, do not believe every spirit, but test the spirits to see whether they are from God, because **many false prophets have gone out into this world.**"

Another example is from the Sermon on the Mount. Jesus warned, in the Gospel of Matthew, chapter seven, verse 15:

> *"**Beware of the false prophets**, who come to you in sheep's clothing, but are inwardly ravenous wolves. You will know them by their fruits. Grapes are not gathered from thorn bushes nor figs from thistles, are they? So every good tree bears good fruit, but the bad tree bears bad fruit. A good tree cannot produce bad fruit, nor can a bad tree produce good fruit."*

Notice the context of Matthew, chapter seven: When Jesus says, "Beware of the false prophets," the context is, "If the tree is good, it bears good fruit. If the tree is bad, it bears bad fruit." So, we are to look at a person's fruit as we watch out for false prophets.

Jesus also tells the church that false prophets will come in looking like one of you. They'll come in looking like "sheep"—like believers. They will come in and join your church and join your worship service and worship right along with you. They will pray over others just like you do. They will show kindness to the people around them. But when you begin to peel back the layers, they are deceptive.

They are not who they are presenting themselves to be — they are "wolves" sent in to devour. That's a stout warning.

Recognizing a Wolf

How do you recognize a "false prophet"? I'm going to give you three things to look for to "test the spirits," as John said, so you can recognize what you're dealing with.

1. Look at their character. Do they have strong, good character?

You may be dealing with a false prophet if the person is arrogant; if they're saying, "I need the mic so that I can say this;" if they throw fits if you won't listen to them or agree to let them speak; or, especially, if they come to you and say, "You're hindering the Holy Spirit by not letting me speak."

Do you know what's so absurd about that? We are *both* in the Holy Spirit. Do you not think that I want a word from God released? If that word is truly from God, don't you think He would tell me, "Listen to this; it's for your church"?

It's a blazing red flag when a prophetic person will not tell you in advance what they want to release. Why would there be a secret word that needs to be given? The only thing I can think of, when a secret word "needs" to be given is if he or she wants to say something negative about the leadership. But, if that's the case, that should be done in private, not in public.

This is not a competition. We're supposed to be in this together. Christ designed us to work together, not in competition to have a word. Legitimate apostolic people know they need prophetic people. They know they need those words, but they can typically also discern a false prophet — someone who is not operating in character, someone who is not operating in the Spirit.

2. Listen to what they prophesy.

Is it in line with God's Word? It has to be—there's no option there. Their word has to be in line with God's word. If they're prophesying over you, "I think you should get a divorce"... well, that's unlikely, unless it lines up with what God says in Scripture about divorce.

Does it seem like the word they are giving is serving the prophet? In other words, the word is actually building up the prophet himself in your eyes?

Does their word bring condemnation or does it bring conviction? This is so important in your Christian walk, you've got to understand it. I'm going to tell you how to know when the enemy is talking to you or when the Holy Spirit is talking to you. It's actually very, very simple, and once you grab a hold of it, you'll understand how to deal with the prophetic.

The Holy Spirit never speaks to you in condemnation: "You are bad." "You are a loser." "You are a sinner." "You might as well give it up." "You messed that up royally." That is *not* the Holy Spirit. That's how the enemy talks to you, with words of condemnation.

The Holy Spirit, and the prophetic voice, will speak to you in words of conviction: "I know there's more for you." "I know God has things for you." "I know that the next time, we're going to do this differently, and it's going to be better." "I'm encouraged that you're going to learn from this and move on." There's a conviction that comes, not a condemnation.

3. This third one has three caveats. The first one:
   - Are they prophesying the obvious?

Do they say something like, "In the next 80 or so days, Jezebel is on the rise, but there will be a trumpet shout"? Duh. No kidding. We know that. We don't need a prophetic word.

   - Are they prophesying the obvious that will happen regularly? "

"I am prophesying that there will be a major shift in the stock market." Yeah, that happens, like, every week… Unfortunately, what they can say is, whenever there's any level of shift, "See, I prophesied that." No, that happens all the time. You're not prophesying anything.

   - Are they using cliché prophetic words?

"I'm here to declare that everything that can be shaken will be shaken." "There is a shift coming in the Spirit." "God is saying, 'see, I'm doing a new thing.'" Yeah, I read that in Scripture, too.

I'm not trying to be mean or critical or harsh here. What I'm saying is sometimes people want to sound prophetic, so they use prophetic terminology. I think it's something to watch for, "Are you just prophesying cliché things so that people will think you're prophetic?"

How Prophetic People Operate

I want to finish by helping you determine if are you designed by Christ to work in the prophetic ministry of the church. We've got to talk about what the prophetic ministry is and what it is not. Here's where you can start applying these things to yourself.

People who work in the prophetic ministry tend to be very righteously-minded. Righteous. "It needs to be done *right*." I'm not talking about control. I'm talking about being "righteously-minded." "Is this being done correctly before God?"

They tend to be very justice-minded. "We need to have some sort of accountability going on."

They tend to be looking for holiness in the church: "Is the church compromising with the world?" "Are we standing firmly on the Word of God?"

They tend to be repentance-minded. "Man, we have got to change our ways. We have got to repent. We've got to go before God and say, 'We're going to turn away from these things and back to You, God.'"

They see rights and wrongs operating in the church, in the leaders and in the group as a whole. They tend to be more black-and-white with how they see issues and they tend to measure things with discernment and a spiritual measuring stick.

Let me give you an example of using a "spiritual measuring stick." Imagine the date on the calendar is December 31, 2023, written as 12-31-23. The prophetic person will say, "Let's see, that's 1-2-3, 1-2-3. So I think in Psalm 123, chapter 12, verse 3, [I'm making this up for the example], it says, 'I will do this thing again.' So, this is a repeat. This is a repeat." Everything they see has got some kind of spiritual significance in numbers or in why it happened. They tend to see spiritual things in everyday circumstances.

I'll give you an example from our body, because Lynn Kercher works in the prophetic. We went down to Bogota, I guess eight or nine years ago. If you haven't noticed, I kind of like cool shirts. On this trip, I went to my cool shirt store, and my cool shirt store didn't have any cool shirts. They had shifted to a new thing, and the new thing was cool jackets. I thought, "I'm not much of a jacket-wearer, but I guess I'll start to wear a few jackets." These things are cheap down there, so I bought two or three of them.

I come out of the mall, I get in the van, and Lynn looks at me and says, "You've got a new mantle today!" I was thinking, "No…, I bought a jacket." But she was saying, "It's a new mantle. God is telling you this is a new mantle, a new season, a new time." And, she was right. The point is, I never thought of that. I just thought, "I'm getting a nice new jacket." But she discerned it spiritually and said, "No, this is a new 'mantle.' This is a shift in who you are." Prophetic people see things that way.

We Are Co-Ministers

The prophetic ministry, remember, is not a title. It doesn't represent some sort of prestigious position. It is not the ultimate authority in the church — Christ is. It is not any more impressive or valuable to the church than the evangelist or the teacher. We are co-ministering in a church. It's not a person that always needs a mic in a church service. It's not a person that must be given a position of prominence or a special seat. It's a ministry that comes with a warning in the New Testament: "Be careful — there are a lot of false prophets out there."

The Downside of the Prophetic Ministry

So let's talk about the downside of being in the prophetic ministry for you individually. What do you need to watch for? What are the traps of being in the prophetic ministry?

- Prophets can sometimes fall into judgmentalism and condemnation.

"I can see wrong things happening. I want to call out wrong; I want to tell people they're doing wrong." That's condemnation. That's not the way God would have you deliver that message, except to those who can receive it in that way, under the right circumstances.

- Prophets sometimes show a lack of grace when dealing with people.

What do I mean? I mean, Prophets, please, don't be so harsh; don't be so direct. Others may need you to have a little softer way to send your message so they can receive it. When you're very harsh and direct, they just get put off by your message, instead of wanting to hear it.

- Prophets often have a negative view toward the body of Christ or toward leaders.

This is because they're called to be the gatekeepers. They're called to declare what's right and wrong, so they often develop a negative view. In other words, they can't see the good that's going on because of what's broken. Therefore, it's easy to develop a critical nature: "My job is to always point out what's not right."

No, sometimes prophets declared what *is* right. Sometimes prophets said, "Yes, God is with you. Go to war. You will win this battle." They were declaring what was right. So I'm just going to say it this way: the goal of the prophetic ministry must be to mentor and develop others, not to break down and condemn others.

The prophetic is a ministry that the church is told to measure and test. We need you. It is important that you speak, but you cannot get easily offended if we say, "Can we take that to prayer?" "Can we ask you to give this to some people who are familiar with the prophetic ministry and let it be measured by them?" That's not an offensive thing to do. That's what Scripture tells us to do.

Walking in Humility

I believe that the main word for the prophetic is humility. When you look at the life of a prophet in the Old Testament, it was never easy. It was always very difficult. One of the most famous Old Testament prophets was Jeremiah. Jeremiah has been called "the weeping prophet."

Why is Jeremiah a weeping prophet? Because Jeremiah sees what's wrong; he knows the hurt that's going to come to the people; he desires for them to turn, so he intercedes for them. He's weeping because he knows what's coming to the people if they don't turn from their sins. I'm telling you, in the church today, we need more prophets who weep.

We don't need another prophet that has a daily podcast, so we can all tune in and see what the "prophetic word for the day" is. What we need are prophets who would weep over the church and say, "God wants us to repent, to change our ways. There are things that God wants to bless us with, and we're withholding those blessings."

By the way, if you're in a prophetic ministry, here's the trap: When you become a prophetic voice and you declare something that is a word from God and people follow it, recognizing the benefit of following your word, what happens next? Those people come back for the next word, which puts pressure on you to have another word, and so on.

Sometimes, then, the flesh creeps in. You think you've got a fresh word, but you're not sure, so you say, "I don't have anything new; I'll just give something generic..." and the next thing you know, you're rolling into a ministry, which is based on, "I've got to have something new on a regular basis because they're coming to me..." That should never be the way the prophetic ministry works.

Are You Called to the Prophetic?

If you believe that you have been designated by Christ to work in the prophetic ministry, Revive Church needs you. We need your words. We need that connection and that design that Christ has made for you in this church.

If you're thinking, "I see things that way. I believe that God is telling me those kinds of things. I think that's a direction I need to move in," we are offering our prophecy class through Heartbeat Discipleship. Sign up for that. Dig into this topic, so you'll understand more of how prophecy operates.

You may be wondering, "Oh, you mean I'm that way because Christ made me that way?" Yeah, you are that way because Christ made you that way. But that doesn't mean you're ready to operate in the prophetic right now, just like the apostle wasn't ready right now. You have to learn humility. You have to learn how to weep for the people. You have to learn how to deliver what you're supposed to deliver, and to keep what you're supposed to keep, and to pray over what you're supposed to pray over, and to hold what you're supposed to hold.

As an apostolic leader in this church, I'm not fighting with the prophetic ministry. I welcome the prophetic. We have a prophetic team that I listen to. When they bring me things, we go to prayer over them. What I want to do, through this series, is resurrect that thing in you to which God has called you. If that's a prophetic ministry, we want that to be developed. We want those words.

If you believe that is stirring up in you, that you might be prophetic, please find a trusted prayer minister and ask them to pray with you. Their prayer will be along the lines of, "God, release to Your child the truth about his prophetic ministry." A prayer counselor will help you discern if this is something you're just feeling, or maybe it's just a desire to control, a desire to have a say in everything. But, maybe you are designed the way Christ designed you, and that's why you see things the way you do.

If the prophetic ministry is the way Christ designed you to contribute to the church, we need your voice. We need your words. We cannot accomplish everything we're supposed to accomplish if we don't listen. But, please don't be offended if we step back and say, "Let's make sure that was from God," because that's the warning we're given to do.

Father God, in the name of Jesus, we're looking to explore everything that You have called for us to be as a church and as individuals. We want the common good to come forward so that we can equip the saints for the work of service, so that we can build up the body of Christ, so that we can attain a unity of this faith, so that we can have a full knowledge of the Son of God and be mature to the measure of the stature which belongs to the fullness of Christ. We can only do that if we're all fully operating in what You have designed us to operate in. Speak to us.
In Jesus' name, Amen.

RESURRECTING EVANGELISTS

As we have stated, at Revive Church, we believe in the five ministries that Christ has given to the church, and we're interested in re-activating those ministries where they have been neglected. Resurrecting evangelists is the topic for this chapter. Chapters one and two dealt with resurrecting apostles and resurrecting prophets, respectively.[15]

The basis of this teaching comes from the Apostle Paul's letter to the Ephesians, chapter four, verses 11-13:

> **"And He [Christ] gave some as apostles, and some as prophets, and some as evangelists, and some as pastors and teachers**, for the equipping of the saints, for the work of service, to the building up of the body of Christ; until we all attain to the unity of the faith, and of the knowledge of the Son of God, to a mature man, to the measure of the stature which belongs to the fullness of Christ."

Those are the five ministries that we are studying. Our focus in this chapter is on evangelists.

---

[15] Based on the message, "Resurrecting Evangelists," August 18, 2024. https://reviveusnow.com/watch

What is an Evangelist?

What does the word "evangelist" mean? What is an evangelist? If you look at the Greek word for "evangelist," it means "a bringer of good tidings." Biblically, an evangelist is someone who is bringing the good news of Jesus Christ, the gospel of salvation and of the Kingdom—a bringer of good tidings. It would only make sense that you must have evangelists in the church: you must have someone sharing the gospel to bring people to Christ so that we can function in the Kingdom.

But, let's be honest—most evangelists make me feel guilty. Why do they make me feel guilty? Because they're sharing the gospel all the time; they're comfortable taking every opportunity to share the gospel; they're bold about sharing the gospel. Anytime, anywhere, with anyone, they will stop and share the gospel! It makes me feel inadequate as a Christian, because I know the gospel, but I don't seem to be quite as bold and "always on" as they are. Many of us may feel like we're not good enough Christians, when compared to what the evangelists are doing.

I believe there's Scriptural support for feeling this way. It's found in the Gospel of Mark, chapter 16, verse 15:

> And He [Jesus] said to them [that is, to His disciples, but it's also to us], ***"Go into all the world and preach the gospel to all creation."***

There it is! If we're not going into *all the world* and preaching the gospel *to all creation*, then we're not doing what Jesus said. Eek!

I don't think there's any doubt—I mean, I really could go dig up a ton of Scripture and roll it all out to you here—that every one of us, as a believer, is supposed to be telling other people about Jesus. We're supposed to be talking about the fact that He came and was crucified on a cross to pay the consequences, the punishment, for our sins; so that whoever would repent and believe in Him could spend an eternity with God. That's the gospel—the "good news;" and, Jesus told us *all* to go and share that with the world.

If it's true that all of us are supposed to be sharing the gospel, why do we need evangelists? What's the point of having an evangelist if all of us share that responsibility? We need to talk about, "What is the ministry of the evangelist?"

Philip the Evangelist

There are several evangelists highlighted in the New Testament. Probably the most famous one is Philip, a disciple who was led to evangelize an Ethiopian eunuch. We have the story in the Book of the Acts of the Apostles, chapter eight, verses 26-38.

> But **an angel of the Lord spoke to Philip saying, "Get up and go south to the road that descends from Jerusalem to Gaza."** (This is a desert road.) So he got up and went; and there was an Ethiopian eunuch, a court official of Candace, queen of the Ethiopians, who was in charge of all her treasure; and he had come to Jerusalem to worship, and he was returning and sitting in his chariot, and was reading the prophet Isaiah. **Then the Spirit said to Philip, "Go up and join this chariot."** Philip ran up and heard him reading Isaiah the prophet, and said, "Do you understand what you are reading?" And he said, "Well, how could I, unless someone guides me?" And he invited

> Philip to come up and sit with him. Now the passage of Scripture which he was reading was this:
>
> "HE WAS LED AS A SHEEP TO SLAUGHTER; AND AS A LAMB BEFORE ITS SHEARER IS SILENT, SO HE DOES NOT OPEN HIS MOUTH. "IN HUMILIATION HIS JUDGMENT WAS TAKEN AWAY; WHO WILL RELATE HIS GENERATION? FOR HIS LIFE IS REMOVED FROM THE EARTH."
>
> The eunuch answered Philip and said, "Please tell me, of whom does the prophet say this? Of himself or of someone else?" Then Philip opened his mouth, and **beginning from this Scripture he preached Jesus to him**. ...

Interesting. I'll make this point several times as we go: notice that it said the evangelist "preached Jesus to him."

> ... As they went along the road they came to some water; and the eunuch said, "Look! Water! What prevents me from being baptized?" And Philip said, "If you believe with all your heart, you may." And he answered and said, **"I believe that Jesus Christ is the Son of God."** And he ordered the chariot to stop; and they both went down into the water, Philip as well as the eunuch, and he baptized him.

This is what we know about this story: Philip shares with the eunuch, starting in the Book of Isaiah. He only has the Hebrew Scriptures to reference—what we call the "Old Testament." Philip goes through the Old Testament, showing the eunuch how Jesus is the Messiah who would come and who would make salvation available.

The eunuch understands it — he receives it — and says, "Hey, what hinders me from being baptized?" Philip says, "Nothing. If you believe, then let's do this." And they stop, and he baptizes him on the spot.

Then later, in Acts, chapter 21 — we went from Acts, chapter eight to Acts, chapter 21 — we are reminded that Philip, in that day, was known as an evangelist. It says in chapter 21, verse eight,

> On the next day we left and came to Caesarea, and **entering the house of Philip the evangelist, who was one of the seven**, and we stayed with him.

I see two things to point out about Philip. First, this was a ministry that Philip is known for. He is known at that time, in the first-century church, at the very beginning of the Church Age, as an evangelist. They call him "Philip the evangelist." He's listed as an evangelist. Christ gave to the church evangelists, and Philip is one of those evangelists.

Secondly, Philip got instruction from the Holy Spirit to share the gospel. The Holy Spirit told him, "Get up and go south to that road that goes from Jerusalem to Gaza." And he does. When he gets there, the Holy Spirit says, "Now go up and get in that chariot." I want you to remember that the Holy Spirit told him to do that.

Other Evangelists

There are other evangelists listed in the New Testament. Some of them we don't even recognize as evangelists. How many of you know that Timothy, in the Bible, whom Paul mentored, was an evangelist? Let's look at that in Paul's second letter to Timothy, chapter four, verses one through five. Here, Paul is giving instructions to Timothy, and I want you to notice especially the language Paul uses at the beginning of this statement:

> "**I solemnly charge you [Timothy] in the presence of God and of Christ Jesus**, who is to judge the living and the dead, and by His appearing and His kingdom:..."

To me, this sounds like Paul is about to lay something heavy down on Timothy. "I solemnly charge you in the presence of God and Christ Jesus..." Whatever he's about to say is an emphatic word.

> "...preach the word; be ready in season and out of season; reprove, rebuke, exhort, with great patience and instruction. For the time will come when they will not endure sound doctrine; but wanting to have their ears tickled, they will accumulate for themselves teachers in accordance to their own desires, and will turn away their ears from the truth and will turn aside to myths. But you [Timothy], be sober in all things, endure hardship, **do the work of an evangelist, fulfill your ministry.**"

I don't know if you saw it, but Paul just said, "Timothy, fulfill your ministry by doing the work of an evangelist."

What do we learn from Timothy as an evangelist? First, we see that he was instructed to do other things, along with sharing the gospel as an evangelist, which was his ministry. What were those other things? "Preach the word." Paul told Timothy to preach the word and to be ready "in season and out of season," to "reprove, rebuke, exhort with great patience and instruction." What is this evangelist told to do to fulfill his ministry? Preach.

But, let's take the whole thing in context: Why did Paul tell Timothy to preach the word? Because people will get to a place where they don't want to hear sound doctrine. The apostle just told the evangelist, "I need you to preach the word because they need sound doctrine."

Do you recall from the first chapter our discussion about the difference between teaching and preaching? Teaching is when we take this basis of information and dissect it in a way that others can understand it, and we transfer that understanding to other people. It's taking that knowledge and allowing people to comprehend what's there.

Preaching, on the other hand, is when someone takes the information he has and then motivates you to use it. I'm going to preach so that you will take what we know we're supposed to do, and that you will actually be convicted to go and do it. That's preaching. That's what evangelists do. They preach the word; they entice; they motivate; they motivate you to accept Christ as Savior.

Paul's Example

Even the apostle Paul shows us what it's like to be an evangelist. In his first letter to the Corinthians, chapter nine, verses 19-23, he describes several key features. This is from the New International Version of the Bible. Paul writes,

> "Though I am free and belong to no one, I have made myself a slave to everyone, to win as many as possible. To the Jews I became like a Jew, to win the Jews. To those under the law I became like one under the law (though I myself

am not under the law), so as to win those under the law. To those not having the law I became like one not having the law (though I am not free from God's law but am under Christ's law), so as to win those not having the law. To the weak I became weak, to win the weak. **I have become all things to all people so that by all possible means I might save some.** I do this for the sake of the gospel that I might share in its blessing."

Wow. What do I learn about being an evangelist from Paul in this set of Scriptures?

- Sometimes you will have to relate to the people with whom you want to share the gospel.

Evangelists are comfortable going where they've got to go to share the gospel. Evangelists are comfortable being with whom they've got to be in order to share the gospel. They take on the environment of the lost in order to win some to Christ—not joining the world, but entering that world, in order that they might rescue some from that world.

- The evangelist sees the torment involved in being lost and the reward involved in being saved.

An evangelist measures what your life is like without Christ and then what it would be like with Christ. Evangelists know that if you are suffering, you can be set free from that suffering. Evangelists know that what you need is what Jesus Christ offers you.

- Evangelists know that their heart is for the lost, and they're willing to do, and easily can do, whatever it takes to win the lost for Jesus.

Evangelists are willing to give things up to gain one soul for the Kingdom. Evangelists are thrilled and fulfilled when someone receives Jesus. Evangelists do not measure the cost that it bears on their own life to share the gospel, to bring someone else to Christ. Actually, they don't even feel like they're sacrificing in any way. Why not? Because it's exciting, and it's necessary to share the gospel! So, they're all in.

The Ministry of the Evangelist

Let's talk about what evangelists look like in the church today. In the charismatic church, we view evangelists as these dynamic people who work in signs, wonders and miracles. We probably think that because it's Scriptural. Going back to what we read in the Gospel of Mark, chapter 16, starting at verse 15 and continuing through verse 20, we read,

> And He [Jesus] said to them, *"Go into all the world and preach the gospel to all creation. He who has believed and has been baptized shall be saved; but he who has disbelieved shall be condemned. **These signs will accompany those who have believed**: in My name they will cast out demons, they will speak with new tongues; they will pick up serpents, and if they drink any deadly poison, it will not hurt them; they will lay hands on the sick, and they will recover."*
>
> So then, when the Lord Jesus had spoken to them, He was received up into heaven and sat down at the right hand of God. **And they went out and preached everywhere, while the Lord**

worked with them, and confirmed the word by the signs that followed.

So we put these together, and we say, "When you are preaching the word, when you are sharing the gospel, signs will follow." That Scripture indicates that these "signs," which by Greek definition, are actually the "miracles and wonders" that can confirm that someone is sent by God, will happen while you're preaching this gospel.

I do believe it's true that that happens for evangelists, but I don't believe it's limited to evangelists. Why do I say that? Because it is true that, in this Scripture, it says, "Go out into the world and preach the gospel," and, at the end, it says that the gospel will be confirmed by the signs that followed. But it also says, "These signs will accompany *those who believe* that gospel."

It says both that the signs will confirm the word that they're preaching, so everyone will know that they are sent by God, and that those who believed in that word will operate in signs.

What are some indications that you might operate in the ministry of the evangelist? See if any of these characteristics resonate with you:

- You see people as "saved" or "lost."
- You are always looking for the opportunity to weave Jesus into the conversation.
- You wonder why other Christians don't have the same level of desire to share the gospel that you do.
- You see sharing the gospel as simple and easy, and it seems that other people are just making too big a deal about it. They just need to go do it.

- Sometimes you struggle with the organized church body because you believe *everyone* should be out sharing the gospel like you're designed to do.
- You know there's always a good time to bring Jesus into the conversation.

How many of you have been out to lunch with that person that always stops and asks the waiter or waitress, "Is there something I can pray for you for?"? Then they'll go into a "Holy Ghost moment" right in the middle of the restaurant? There's nothing wrong with that at all, but you were thinking to yourself, "Well, I might have asked if we could meet after work and talk to them privately; I don't want to put them on the spot…"

Evangelists don't care about putting anybody on the spot! They care about you meeting Jesus and entering His kingdom.

A lot of evangelists will carry little knickknacks or gospel tracts, if you're my age, to start a conversation. These days, it's a penny with a cross cut out of the center. They'll give it to you and say, "Jesus just makes sense." Or, they'll leave little crosses at the table—anything to open the conversation.

These people are fun and exciting to be around. You just want to go out with them to see what they're going to do next!

Some Words of Caution

There are things we need to consider when it comes to being an evangelist. If you feel like I'm talking to you, like I'm describing you, I want you to hear these things as well:

- Evangelists tend to project evangelism onto everyone.

They tend to believe that everyone should feel like they do about sharing the gospel. They may also feel like anyone who *doesn't* feel like they do about sharing the gospel just doesn't get it yet; that somehow they don't love Jesus, or want to save souls, if they don't have the same desire that an evangelist has.

By the way, if we are all supposed to be evangelists, then why did Christ give the church apostles, prophets, pastors and teachers? Why didn't He just make us all evangelists?

- Evangelists often neglect the discipleship of the people they bring to Christ.

They're out there to heal; they're out there to save; they're out there to deliver; and, then, they move on to the next person who needs Christ.

They forget that people need to be further discipled after their conversion. People need to learn who they are—their identity—in Christ. They need to learn their authority over the demonic. They need to be encouraged and built up and consoled.

People who become new believers need a family of believers around them. They have questions. There are 66 books in the Bible—that's a lot of information! The new believer can be like, "What do I do with this? 'Thee,' 'thou,' 'shalt,' 'begat,' 'begat,' 'begat'—I don't know what to do with all this information."

They need pastoring. When the enemy brings chaos into their lives, they may say, "Wait a minute! The evangelist told me everything was going to be great when I received Christ, and now it's going bad. What's the deal?"

They need teachers to help them understand the Word of God and how to apply it. So again, I ask, if sharing the gospel is the only important thing for every believer, then why did Christ give us pastors and teachers?

- Evangelists may find operating in miracles, signs and wonders tempting and get off into the flesh.

It's an exciting life—exciting things happen when people are getting saved. Many evangelists take what we call "the itinerant route," where they travel; they do crusades; they do events; they do conferences. It's not about the specific church body where they're presenting—it's about moving on to the next event. They can become disconnected from the church body, if they're not careful. I'm not saying all of them do—I'm not passing this over the entire group—but many of them get disconnected from the church and take on a bit of a showmanship mentality.

They feel they have to dress a certain way, and make sure they have a sweat rag to wipe their brow. They have to get a crowd all worked up and excited so they can lay hands on them and people can fall down.

If you don't mind my saying to the evangelists who've operated in that direction, I say this kindly and lovingly: If you have to video and take pictures and post them of what happened when you evangelized, then it's more about you than it is about the gospel. There's a big difference in filming what you said and filming the testimonies of the people affected by what you said. One of them says, "I need a camera so everybody can see what I'm doing." The other one says, "Look at what God did in that person." "I want to hear their testimony."

- Evangelism often can move into what I call "bad methods."

I don't happen to believe that going to a big city and standing on a street corner with a bullhorn, yelling, "Everyone, repent!" is a good method of evangelism

Preaching condemnation and repentance as the way to come to Christ, as in, "You are going to hell if you don't accept the message I'm sending today," may be preaching truth, but you've got a delivery problem. That's not a good method.

If you're continuing to push people after they have rejected the gospel, that's a problem. When I was in my twenties, I was in a church, in a denomination that starts with "B" and ends with "T" and has a "P" in the middle. We had a program called "Continuous Witness Training." It was a way to walk through a gospel presentation with someone.

After we had gone through the training, they sent us out in groups of two: someone "senior," who knew what they were doing, with someone like me, the "rookie." We literally walked into neighborhoods and knocked on doors, hoping to witness to people.

We came to this one house, and my leader asked the person, "Do you know Christ as your Savior?" She said, "Yes, I do! I've been a Christian for years." He said, "Well, okay, if you don't mind, we're in the middle of training Todd how to present the gospel. Can we come in and present it so that he can observe me presenting it?" She said, "Yeah, I'd be okay with that."

So, we go into her living room, we sit down on the couches and chairs around a coffee table, and my leader "takes off," going through the material, explaining Christ, the whole bit. He gets down to the point where it's decision time, looks at the lady and says, "Are you willing to accept Christ today?" She just looks at him and smiles and says, "As I said, I already have." Then he said, "No. Do you understand that the blood of Christ saves you, and that you have to accept that over your life?" And she said, "Yes, I do." And he said, "But have you done that? Have you repented of..." And she finally looked at him and said, "If your goal was to come here today to annoy me, you have succeeded. But, I've told you, I've already accepted Christ as my Savior."

At that moment, what hit me so hard was how, in our zeal to evangelize, we can be obnoxious people with an absolutely wrong approach. We need to stop and ask, "Am I sharing the gospel here, or am I trying to finish the plan of the program that I've been presented?"

God's Great Purpose

Why do we have this ministry of evangelists? Why did Christ give evangelists to the church? I'm going to say this very bluntly, and it may not be the answer you would think I would give to this question. Why did Christ give the church evangelists? I believe it is because God knows that what the church also needed was apostles, prophets, pastors and teachers.

Why did He give us evangelists? He gave us evangelists because somebody was going to have to teach those people who believed, and somebody was going to have to pastor those people who believed. Somebody was going to have to lead and organize what was going on in the Kingdom, and someone was going to have to prophesy.

When we look back at our baseline Scripture from Ephesians, chapter four, verses 11-13, it said He gave evangelists…

> "**...for the equipping of the saints for the work of service, to the building up of the body of Christ;** until we all attain to the unity of the faith, and of the knowledge of the Son of God, to a mature man, to the measure of the stature which belongs to the fullness of Christ."

If we don't have these other positions, then who builds up, trains up and prepares the people that the evangelist leads to Christ? We have to have evangelists. We have to have somebody sharing the gospel, including us, but somebody designed to do it, and then we have to have these other ministries around them.

Things to Remember

If you're working in the ministry of the evangelist—if you know, "Yeah, I'm an evangelist"—there are some things to remember:

1. Be Holy Spirit-led.

Yes, you have a call to share the gospel. Yes, Jesus gave you that ministry, gave you that desire, gave you that excitement. Yes, there are lost souls to be saved. Yes, Jesus is what they need. But remember, it's God's kindness that leads us to repentance.[16] We need to join that leading of the Spirit; we need to be led by the Spirit. When Philip was dealing with the eunuch, he was led two separate times: "Get up and go south to the road…" and "Go up and join that chariot." He was led by the Holy Spirit. Remember to be led by the Spirit.

---

[16] Romans 2:4

2. What you do is important; it is righteous; it is necessary; but, so is the work of discipleship.

Remember that Jesus told the apostles, "Go and make disciples." After someone comes to Christ, they will need someone to raise them up. I say this kindly, only because I've had to experience it myself: If you are an evangelist, do not disrespect the other ministries given to the church. Often evangelists see their ministry as the most important, and everything else is lesser than what the evangelist does.

3. Remember that you have a special calling that not everyone else has.

We are not all like you, and we should not all be like you. Don't get frustrated with others when they're not like you.

4. Know your doctrine.

You don't get a pass on knowing the Word of God and the doctrines of God just because you're sharing the gospel. Your presentation must be Biblical. The people you present to may have questions that you're going to have to answer. You've got to know the Word of God.

Let's think about it for a moment: Where in the Bible was anyone brought to Christ by repeating a prayer? It doesn't exist. Where in the Bible was anyone told to "ask Jesus into your heart?" I'm not saying these things are wrong or bad and that you can't use them. I'm saying, we've got to think about it.

I heard a 7-year-old girl one time tell me, "I did not want to invite Jesus into my heart because He's a big man, and it would hurt." It's a matter of recognizing your audience and what they know and what they understand, then presenting Biblical truth to them. These things aren't wrong, but you've got to have an understanding of what you're actually presenting.

    5. Don't sacrifice the relationships in your life and justify it because you're saving souls.

What do I mean by that? You still have to be a good spouse. Biblically, you're called to it. You still have to be a good parent. Biblically, you're called to it. You still have to be a good friend. You are not a one-man show. You are part of a larger body, an organization that supports what you do. You're being arrogant if you decide you don't need the body of Christ and everybody should just be out on the streets.

    6. Know that you may not be ready today to fulfill the desire that God has put in your heart.

Maybe you're not doctrinally ready. You may need some training. In my past, as the senior pastor of a church, I recognized that I didn't have a solid enough Biblical understanding of the gospel. I could explain a lot of things in Scripture, but I didn't have confidence that I could sit down and lay out how this whole thing happens Biblically.

So, I went to what was called a "Gospel Bootcamp" at Spanish River, led by "Pastor David." He has passed away now, but at the time, I went to his home on a Friday night, and for four hours, he Biblically laid out the gospel for me and seven others. He instructed us, "This is what the gospel is. This is how it works. This is how it's applied. This is the understanding of the Biblical presentation."

Then we came back on Saturday, and for eight hours — there were eight of us — each one of us had to take an hour presenting the gospel over and over, while he critiqued it, until we each got it to the point that it was truly Biblical and clear.

Am I saying that you can't just go tell someone that Jesus loves them, and He wants to step into their life, and they can accept Him and receive His forgiveness? No, I'm not saying that. You absolutely can. Let the Holy Spirit be in charge, in the hour, of what you are to say.

But that does not excuse us from understanding what the Bible says about salvation and about presenting the gospel. Be ready. Maybe, if you believe your call is itinerant, that you're going to be going places, that there are going to be crusades, and there are going to be conferences, then maybe you already know what you're going to say—you're prepared in that way—but you may not know what it takes to set up a crusade, on a soccer field, with a sound system and lights and provision for rain, with some food and some safety and some security, and what all has to be done around that to make it happen. So, maybe there's some more training you need to go through.

Whether it's on the street or whether you're in a crusade environment, there are some requirements that you may need to learn in order to be ready. That's not saying you can't share the gospel today. I'm saying, if you're going to step out into the ministry of the evangelist, you need to be prepared.

Your Incredible Value to the Kingdom

Evangelists are incredibly valuable to the kingdom of God. They are not odd; they are not fanatical; they are not radical. They are operating in the ministry and in the desires given to them by Christ.

Evangelists have so much to teach us about how to share the gospel. We can learn so much from going out with them and just watching them, because they're anointed and gifted to do this thing. We may not be so gifted in this area, so we need to see the process in action. Evangelists, we need to hear you. We need to learn from you.

We also need to invest in evangelists. From an apostolic side, they need to be invested in. An evangelist needs to be invested in because that evangelist's return of bringing people into the kingdom of God is higher than the average person working in a different ministry.

We all have a mandate to share the gospel, we all know that. But evangelists are designed by God to bring the lost into the Kingdom. If we don't give them a place, if we don't give them the support, then they want to leave the church body and go do it on their own. The rest of us shouldn't get offended because their return may be higher in the Kingdom.

Evangelists remind us about the mission that we're all on: to bring people out of the kingdom of darkness into the kingdom of light, to bring people out of their suffering and out of their torment into the joy and peace of the kingdom of God.[17]

Evangelists have a passion that we all admire. There are times when I just look at them and say, "I wish I had thought of that." "I wish I could do that." "I wish I was comfortable the way they're comfortable." They're exciting people to be around, because they're doing something which, in our core, we know *we* need to be doing—sharing the gospel. When I'm around an evangelist, I'm reminded that I need to be sharing the gospel. I see that this person does it so well, I'm reminded that I've got to learn from him. I want to walk in that path, too. At Revive Church, we are regularly inspired by a gifted

---

[17] Colossians 1:13, John 1:1-5, 9-13

evangelist, Mr. Mike Della Fave. If you want to have an exciting day, go with him to Wawa or Walmart sometime.

"Take This Free Gift"[18]

Jesus is so amazing. When we look to other people, we get disappointed. When we look to ourselves, we get disappointed, for sure. But, when we look to Jesus Christ, He will never disappoint us. It's called being "born again." It's called receiving His love. It's called receiving His forgiveness and His kindness.

Jesus Christ, the Son of God, humbled Himself beyond anyone, ever. It's actually the greatest love story ever. He came down in our likeness, in our form, took the punishment we deserved on a cross, shed His blood and came up in resurrection power, so we can be transformed into His likeness.

There's no other "god" that ever did such a thing! In every other religion, you have to earn it. You do this and do that, do, do, do, while Jesus Christ says, "Take this free gift." Jesus Christ says, "Take this free gift. I did it *all*. All you need to do is receive it."

That's called grace. Without the Holy Spirit, you can't even get saved. Some people say, "I don't know if I'm really saved." Without the Holy Spirit, Jesus is just a figment of the imagination. He's just a fairytale. In the Gospel of John, Jesus Christ said "Salvation is to know God."[19] And that word

---

[18] This portion of the message provided by Mike Della Fave, Children's Director at Revive Church.

[19] John 17:3

"know" refers to an experience. When you get born again, you come into the experience of Jesus Christ and what He did.

The Holy Spirit's major role is to magnify Jesus Christ. He convicts us of our sin. And, I was one of the worst. I drank a lot. I fought a lot. I joined the army to be cool, to be "Mr. Tough Guy," because, in reality, I was rejected my whole life.

Then Jesus Christ completely changed my life. I used to fight, drink, do all this stuff. But, Jesus—when I met Him through an encounter, not a feeling—He changed me; He changed everything. When you just believe God and you receive Him; when you look at His love and kindness and mercy and grace; and you see what He did and you receive Him; it changes everything. It changes your nature.

Now, I'm not perfect! Trust me, "Sergeant Della Fave" came out just this week. But do you know what? Jesus Christ is perfect. When you look to His perfection and receive His grace, there's nothing like it. When you look to the Father's love and realize, "I'm forgiven. I'm accepted. God is proud of me," that's what the gospel is. Pastor Todd said it's the "good news." It is good news. It's not rules. It's not a rule book. It's freedom.

If you want to receive Jesus right now, you just receive it by faith. As Pastor Todd said, there's no special prayer—that's not in the Bible—Jesus says, "Just believe."[20] If you receive Him right now, you are in the kingdom of God. You've humbled yourself, and you've said, "Jesus, I need you. I'm a sinner. I can't do it on my own."

---

[20] Mark 5:36

FIVEFOLD FRAMEWORK

When you stop trying to do things on your own, you can enter the Kingdom. It's called "denying yourself," which is completely opposite of how the world operates. The world wants to get ahead. Everyone wants to be first in line; they want to be in the spotlight; they want to be the one who gets promoted. But, Jesus says, "Deny yourself and trust Me."[21]

Lord Jesus, if anyone wants to receive You right now, we ask that You would "show up." Move in Your kindness and in Your love. The truth of the gospel brings healing. It brings freedom physically and spiritually. We pray that we could just receive that right now.

If that's you, just receive Him as you read this. Just receive Him right now. If you need healing in your body, receive it right now.

Anyone that needs You today, Lord Jesus, I pray that You would seal them right now, in the name of Jesus. Lord, we thank You for new children entering the Kingdom this morning.[22]
We praise you, God. Amen.

---

[21] Luke 9:23

[22] For more information, go to www.reviveusnow.com. Click on "Hello! I'm new to Christ."

Closing Benediction

If you believe that Jesus Christ gave you the ministry of evangelism for the church, we need to know. Maybe you're thinking, "I *think* it's me, but I'm not sure." Maybe you'd like someone to pray with you, to get some level of assurance that, "Yes, that is what I'm called to do." I encourage you to find a trusted prayer partner to pray with you.

You may be struggling in other ways right now. Maybe you're not really sure about the whole Jesus Christ thing. Maybe you are in a place where there's too much going on in your life. You've got struggles in your family, in your finances, with your relationships. You've got struggles inside of you, and you just need some freedom from that. Christ offers that freedom right now. Let someone pray with you. Get that broken off of you so you can walk in more joy and peace.

Father God, in the name of Jesus, we just declare that we're Yours. How You designed us — what You made us to be — we want to walk in the fullness of that. I ask You to come into these readers right now and speak to them about who You made them to be. Release us into what You've called us to do.
In Jesus' name, Amen.

FIVEFOLD FRAMEWORK

RESURRECTING PASTORS

Our discussion of the fivefold ministry has covered the ministries of the apostle, the prophet and the evangelist. Now, we have come to the ministry of the pastor. To clarify what we're talking about in this chapter, when we're referring to pastors, we're not talking about people who lead churches. That's not what we're talking about here. The pastor of your church may, in fact, work in the apostolic ministry, may work in the prophetic, may be an evangelist or may be a teacher.[23]

That term, "pastor of a church," as in, people call me "Pastor Todd," is something the church uses as a title for someone who "oversees a flock," or who gives direction to a group of believers that meet together. But that's not what we're talking about in this chapter.

Here, we're talking about the ministry of the pastor. There are pastors who may or may not oversee an actual flock of believers. There is a ministry of the pastoral, and you may very well be called into that. That's what we want to explore here.

---

[23] Based on the message, "Resurrecting Pastors," August 25, 2024. https://reviveusnow.com/watch

The Apostle Paul tells us, in his letter to the Ephesians, chapter four, verses 11-13,

> **"And He [Christ] gave some as apostles, and some as prophets, and some as evangelists, and some as pastors and teachers**, for the equipping of the saints for the work of service, to the building up of the body of Christ; until we all attain to the unity of the faith and of the knowledge of the Son of God, to a mature man, to the measure of the stature which belongs to the fullness of Christ."

That's a big mouthful right there, but that's why we're given these five ministries: in order to build us up, until we attain unity in the faith.

What does this Scripture say a pastor is within the fivefold ministry? The Greek word is *poimen,* and it is used throughout the New Testament. The Greek definition of that word is a "herdsman," someone who herds or shepherds animals. As that word, *poimen,* is used, all throughout the New Testament, only one time is it translated as "pastor," and that's here, in Ephesians, chapter four. The remainder of the time, *poimen* is translated as "shepherd."

Therefore, the basic definition of the word "pastor" is "shepherd." In our ordinary use of the word, we are referring to a person that gives guidance to a group of believers. That's our topic for this chapter: those of you who are called to be "shepherds." To begin, let's discover the basis for this term in the Bible.

The Greatest Shepherd of All Time

Who was the all-time greatest and best shepherd-pastor ever? Jesus. Good answer! Jesus is always the answer. Jesus was indeed the Great Shepherd. In the letter to the Hebrews, chapter 13, verses 20-21, the author refers to Jesus as a shepherd:

> "Now the God of peace, who brought up from the dead **the great Shepherd of the sheep** through the blood of the eternal covenant, even Jesus our Lord, equip you in every good thing to do His will, working in us that which is pleasing in His sight, through Jesus Christ, to whom be the glory forever and ever. Amen."

Jesus is the Great Shepherd, called out as the Great Shepherd in Scripture. Conversely, if Jesus is the Great Shepherd, guess what we are? "Sheep."

Jesus Himself creates this imagery for us when He's speaking to His disciples, as recorded in the Gospel of John, chapter 10, verses 14-16. Jesus says,

> *"**I am the good shepherd**, and I know My own and My own know Me, even as the Father knows Me and I know the Father; and **I lay down my life for the sheep.** I have other sheep, which are not of this fold; I must bring them also, and they will hear My voice; and they will become one flock with one shepherd."*

Jesus calls Himself the Good Shepherd. And, those for whom He laid down His life — you and me — are His sheep.

If you're wondering who Jesus is talking about when He says, "You're my sheep, but there's another fold of sheep that I have to bring in," He's talking to the Jews about the Gentiles, who are going to be invited into the kingdom of God. He's saying, "There is another fold of sheep, called the Gentiles, and I will bring them in, too. You will be one flock, with one shepherd." He goes on, in John, chapter 10, verse 27, to say,

> *"My sheep hear My voice, and I know them, and they follow Me."*

Therefore, Jesus is the Good Shepherd and believers are His sheep.

The Ministry of a Shepherd

Scripture calls out for us today that there are shepherds among us. There are pastors among us; they're here to help build up the saints and help us attain unity in the faith.

If you are called to that ministry, it's very simple: You are called to be a shepherd. Jesus was the Great Shepherd. All you have to do is "be like Jesus." Ready? Go!

That's a big task! So, let's talk about what shepherds do. What do shepherds really do?

- They "tend" the flock. They keep their attention on the needs of the sheep.

- They guard the flock. They are always watching for harm that might come from the outside to affect the sheep. They guard the sheep.

- They "herd" the flock. What would that mean, "herding"? They keep the flock together, ensuring that there's no division, ensuring that there's no departure, there's no wandering.

- They make sure the flock is fed. They are constantly taking the flock to greener pastures, making sure they are fed.

This is what shepherds do.

"Feed My Sheep"

Many of the greatest characters in the Bible were actually shepherds. You know them. You remember Cain and Abel. Abel was a shepherd until he was murdered by Cain. David was a shepherd who was anointed as a boy to become the king of Israel. Moses was a shepherd in Midian when he saw the burning bush, and God said, "You're going back to deliver My people out of Egypt."[24]

There are "shepherds" in the Bible that perhaps many of you have never really realized had the ministry of the shepherd. I'm going to bring out one guy who was actually operating in the ministry of the shepherd, although he had another ministry calling as well. (Yes, you can have more than one ministry calling, by the way.)

The Apostle Peter was actually operating in the ministry of a shepherd. I don't know about you, but I don't often think about Peter that way. I think about Peter as the guy who pops off at the mouth a lot and gets in trouble for it by Jesus. He's the one who denied Christ three times,[25] and then Jesus had to come back and work with him after the resurrection. But that's exactly my point.

---

[24] Genesis 4:1-8 / 1 Samuel 16 / Exodus 3

[25] John 18:15-18, 25-27

Let's look at that moment where Christ reinstates Peter. We read in the Gospel of John that Jesus appeared to some of His disciples at the Sea of Galilee after His resurrection. It's at this time that Jesus makes the point of specifically talking to Peter, because of Peter's denial of Him, during His trial and crucifixion.

Listen to what Jesus says in John, chapter 21, verses 15-17:

> So when they had finished breakfast, Jesus said to Simon Peter, *"Simon, son of John, do you love Me more than these?"* He said to Him, "Yes, Lord; You know that I love You." **He [Jesus] said to him, *"Tend My lambs."*** He said to him a second time, *"Simon, son of John, do you love Me?"* He said to Him, "Yes, Lord; You know that I love You." **He said to him, *"Shepherd My sheep."*** He said to him the third time, *"Simon, son of John, do you love Me?"* Peter was grieved because He said to him the third time, "Do you love Me?" And he said to Him, "Lord, You know all things; You know that I love You." **Jesus said to him, *"Tend My sheep."***

This is Jesus, who gave ministries to the church, talking to Peter about his ministry of being a shepherd. He said, "Tend My lambs." What does "tend" mean? Take care of them, feed them. "Shepherd the sheep." What does "shepherd" mean? Be one who oversees the flock, who gathers them, who protects them, who guards them.

Many years later, we can see Peter operating in this ministry of the shepherd, by reading what he wrote in what we call the Book of First Peter, chapter five, verses one through four:

> "Therefore, I [Peter] exhort the elders among you, as your fellow elder and witness of the

sufferings of Christ, and a partaker also of the glory that is to be revealed, **shepherd the flock of God among you, exercising oversight** not under compulsion, but voluntarily, according to the will of God; not for sordid gain, but with eagerness; nor yet as lording it over those allotted to your charge, but **proving to be examples to the flock.** And when the Chief Shepherd appears, you will receive the unfading crown of glory."

These are the words of someone to whom Christ said, "You are a shepherd." Peter goes as a shepherd and speaks to those who are also shepherding and says, "This is how we should shepherd." He says, "You should shepherd your flock, not out of compulsion, but eagerly. Do it voluntarily. Be examples to your flock." I want you to pay attention to the words that a shepherd is using.

"Little Children…"

I also believe that there's another apostle who works in the ministry of the pastor, the Apostle John. What makes me say that? Let's read what John wrote to his followers, to his "flock," in his first letter, "First John," chapter two, verse 18:

> "Children, it is the last hour; and just as you heard **that antichrist is coming**, even now many antichrists have appeared; from this we know that it is the last hour."

In 1 John, chapter three, verse seven, John writes,

> "Little children, **make sure no one deceives you;** the one who practices righteousness is righteous, just as He [God] is righteous."

In his third letter, chapter four, John says,

> "**I have no greater joy than this**, to hear of my children walking in the truth."

Where is John's focus in these things that he's writing? His focus is on the sheep. He's saying, "I want to protect you." "I want you to know that antichrists are coming and deception is coming." "I want you to be led by the truth."

Also notice that John refers to the people he's writing to as "little children." "You're my little children; I'm raising you up; I'm taking care of you." These are words of love, words of endearment, words of kindness. He's showing concern for the people.

Do You Have the Call?

If you're wondering, "Am I called to be a pastor?" think about it in these terms: The bottom line for pastors, acting as shepherds, is they focus on people. They care about people. They care if people are being taken care of. They care if people are in danger. They are willing to sacrifice to help people. They find great satisfaction in making the lives of people better.

Probably, every one of us would say, "Well, I want that to be said about me. I care about people. I want people to be okay. I care that no harm comes to them." That may be true, but the question is: Is this an overwhelming desire in you? Do you think about this on a regular basis? Are you more than a nice person? Could you actually be a pastor instead of just being kind? Is there a ministry there because you care for people?

Often, the ministry of a pastor goes to the extent of being personally affected if the flock around them has needs. They are personally affected when they observe the needs of other people. We see this in Jesus, in the Gospel of Matthew, chapter nine, verse 36:

> "Seeing the people, **He [Jesus] felt compassion for them**, because they were distressed and dispirited like sheep without a shepherd."

Jesus felt compassion for them because it was like they were sheep, and they didn't have a shepherd, and they were dispirited, they were discouraged. That made Him *feel* something; it invoked some emotion within Jesus.

On another occasion, in the Gospel of Luke, chapter 13, verse 34, Jesus cries out:

> *"O Jerusalem, Jerusalem, the city that kills the prophets and stones those sent to her!* **How often I wanted to gather your children together**, *just as a hen gathers her brood under her wings, and you would not have it!"*

This is Jesus expressing His emotion over the people. "I want to protect you. I wish you would come under My wings."

My point in these Scriptures is to hear the pastoral words of Jesus: He felt compassion because the people were distressed and dispirited. He wanted to "gather them under His wings," like a mother hen, to protect them. These are words of emotion brought about by the struggles of the people the shepherd oversees.

In other words, when people are troubled and struggling, a pastor becomes troubled and struggles. He has compassion. He begins to say, "How can I work with them?" "How can I help them?" "How can I solve this problem?"

You might be feeling the call to the ministry of a pastor if you find yourself very emotionally attached to a lot of people; if you have compassion and empathy for what's going on in their lives; if you feel people need help and *you* want to be the person who helps them; if you feel maintaining a relationship with people is of high and great importance; and, if you see people hurt even when they're not expressing it.

Pastors have the ability to look at people and say, "They're suffering; they're hurting. I can feel it. I can tell. I know they're struggling with something, and I want to go talk to them about it."

A pastor desires for everyone to feel included and loved. "I don't want anyone to feel outcast. I don't want anybody to feel like we don't want them to be a part of us. I want to draw them in."

Pastors often speak in words of emotion. They speak in words of the soul. As we read before, John says, "I have no greater joy than to hear my little children are walking in the truth." Peter says, "I want you to volunteer with eagerness. I want you to *want* to do this." Jesus shows His emotion by saying, "I felt compassion on them because I wanted to protect them. I wanted to bring them in."

The way I most often identify someone who is operating in the ministry of the pastor is by their vocabulary. You can hear it in their words. For instance, when you're in a group of people praying, I can tell you who's operating in the ministry of the pastor just by the words they use in their prayers. They pray with words of the soul. They pray with emotion.

Even when Jesus is talking about the opposite side of shepherding—when someone is not a genuine shepherd—you can feel His emotion. Let's look back at John, chapter 10, verse 12:

> *"He who is a hired hand, and not a shepherd, who is not the owner of the sheep, sees the wolf coming, and*

leaves the sheep and flees, and the wolf snatches them and scatters them."

He's saying, "If you're a good shepherd, you don't run away." Christ says, "I am with you always as a shepherd."[26]

"The Lord is My Shepherd"

I'm going to take you to the writing of a shepherd, and I want you to look at it differently than maybe you've looked at it in the past. I want you to look for the writing of a shepherd. What words does the shepherd use? What is he trying to get across?

The shepherd I'm talking about, of course, is David, and the writing is so very familiar to you: the 23rd Psalm. Remember, David is a shepherd, and this is what he says:

> The Lord is my shepherd,
> I shall not want.

He speaks of the Lord meeting all of his needs.

> He makes me lie down in green pastures;
> He leads me beside quiet waters.

These are poetic words speaking about the rest that we need and the peace that we have when we are with the Lord.

> He restores my soul;...

This is the restoration of what is broken inside of him. The Lord puts it back together for us and gives us guidance.

> He guides me in the paths of righteousness
> For His name's sake.

---

[26] Matthew 28:20

> Even though I walk through the valley of the
> shadow of death,
> I fear no evil, for You are with me;...

David speaks about the peace that he has and how he has no fear. Why? Because God is with him. Referring to the comfort given to him, he says,

> ...Your rod and Your staff, they comfort me.
> You prepare a table before me in the presence
> of my enemies;...

He's speaking of the Lord's provision and protection.

> ...You have anointed my head with oil;...

David is pointing out the intimacy and the personal nature of the calling and the anointing. Talking about the abundance in the Lord, he adds,

> ...My cup overflows.
> Surely goodness and lovingkindness will
> follow me all the days of my life,...

Is that not an interesting thing for a person to say? "Surely goodness and lovingkindness are going to follow me." This is a person who's very much in touch with his emotions. "Goodness and kindness are important, and they're going to follow me all the days of my life."

> ...And I will dwell in the house of the Lord
> forever.

David makes clear his feelings: "I am safe. I am secure. I am locked in with the Lord forever."

Do you recognize the words of a pastor? These are words of personal connection, words of peace, relationship, rest, comfort and caring.

Now, I'm not saying that the rest of us don't care about people, but when you listen to a pastor speak, he is reaching into your soul. He's trying to touch your emotions. He is trying to relate to you so that he can offer help to you.

Pastors often ask you, "Are you doing okay?" Pastors say things like, "Is there anything I can do for you?" Their favorite phrases of all time are, "Talk to me." "Can we talk?" "Do you want to sit down and talk?" "Let's process through what's going on with you."

Pastors speak in terms of people being tended to, people being guarded, people being protected and provided for, people being "fed." Why? Because that's what shepherds do.

We Need the Pastoral Ministry

Pastors are beautiful in the body of Christ. They are critical and important. There's not just one pastor in Revive Church. There are not 10 pastors in this church. I'll guarantee you, there are 50 or more pastors in this church! The pastoral ministry is such a critical role in the church that we end up being inundated with pastors.

Why does God give so many people the ministry of being a pastor? In simple terms, I believe it's because pastors make us all feel more human. They tend to make us feel more loving and caring, by the way they treat people. They remind us that everyone around us is just a person who's looking for peace in their life, who's looking for love in their life, who may have some needs that we can meet. They remind us that Christ was loving and caring to the people around Him.

If that's your call, we need you. If those words hit you and you said, "I'm that way. I can't help it, when I see somebody hurting, I just want to go and say, 'What's going on with you?

I want to be able to help you. How can I take care of you?'" we need you.

Or, maybe, when you see somebody going down a path that's not good for them, you just want to step in and say, "Stop! This is not going to lead you to a good place. Let me help you. Do you want to talk? Can we sit down? I just see that you're feeling stressed and I want to talk you through it." If that's hitting you, maybe the calling on your life is actually pastoring.

Be Aware

In this series, I'm trying to advise each of us of the downsides of each of the ministries in the fivefold ministry. These are areas for you to be aware of, if you feel you're called to be a pastor.

1. Pastors have a tendency to become "all things to all people."

If you're identified as a pastor, everybody will contact you for the problems they have, because they know you're available to help. Unfortunately, you won't be the expert in everything they need.

As a pastor, sometimes you have to figure out that holding their hand does not solve their bad financial decisions. You may find out that praying with them and being with them during the domestic abuse also needs legal action.

You'll need to know, as a pastor, when to hand a person off to someone who's more knowledgeable than you. Maybe they need to be handed off to someone apostolic, to figure out their financial mess. Maybe they need to be handed off to a teacher so they can understand righteousness from the Word.

I believe, generally, "tough love" is very difficult for pastors. It's very difficult to say, "Enough, enough, I need you to stop what you're doing." Tough love can be difficult because there is a definitive line between helping and enabling.

Ask the question this way: Do you know someone who spends years in counseling because they're being sustained by the counseling and not being equipped to move past whatever the issue is? In other words, you've got to know as a pastor when to say, "I cannot continue this because you are not changing, and you're depending on me to just carry you through. I've tried to equip you, but you're not becoming equipped."

Finally, recognize when all your helpfulness is meeting *your* need to help someone and you're not actually meeting *the other person's* need.

2. Pastors can get overwhelmed with too many people that need your help.

There are still only 24 hours in a day and still only seven days in a week. There are many, many, many people who need pastoring. If you are always available, there are many, many, many people who will call you. Turn that phone off at night.

I say it this way to pastors I know and to my own staff: Protect your longevity. The church doesn't need more pastors who do an amazing job for two years, burn out, lose their family, and say, "I was a mess."

3. Pastors may tend to hold back other pastors from pastoring by believing they are the best at what they do.

Pastors sometimes have a hard time giving other pastors the opportunity because they're used to being in the forefront.

Their desire to do what God called them to do may not allow other pastors to do what God called *them* to do.

There are more pastors than just the lead pastor in a church. Pastors are told to rest. Pastors are told to consider one another. One of the things that can happen is that pastors aren't recognizing that Jesus is always the Great Shepherd for His people. Jesus will always be their Messiah. You do not have to be their Messiah, which leads to my next point.

4. Pastors can get a Messiah complex as they help and as they minister.

One of the most difficult things to deal with when you're helping people is the feedback of how much you helped them. "You were amazing! I tell you, you just broke stuff off me, right and left. I just feel so good when I talk to you. I just want to recommend you to everybody." All of a sudden, you start believing how important you are.

A mentor of mine, years ago—he's passed on to eternity now—said this: "When you get feedback, take 100% of the feedback you get and throw out the bottom 20%. That's the bad stuff. They're just being mean. Don't listen to it. But, do not forget to throw out the top 20% also! They're just flattering you and trying to butter you up. Believe what's in the middle. Believe that you are average."

Talk about a motivator to become better when somebody says, "You need to believe you're average"! "Well, I ain't staying average...!" My point is, with the Messiah complex, you begin to believe how important you are. You begin to believe that because you're good at pastoring, you need to become a professional counselor.

I spoke with a professional counselor I know and he said, "You'd be stunned at how many people believe they should go into counseling, because they have ministered to people well, and yet, those are two completely different ballgames."

You can believe that you know how to meet everyone's needs, and you can believe that you're better at it than those around you. You can desire, "Everyone needs to know I'm better at this, so that they will send people to me." You can try to take the place and the role the Great Shepherd should have in their lives.

5. Pastors need to count the cost.

You need to count the cost of your desire to help others against the desire to minister to your own family. Too much time with others makes a family feel neglected and unimportant. You will enjoy helping others, but you may not consider how much time you're taking away from your family to do that.

Knowing how much you're helping others is not justification for neglecting your family and friends. Jesus, the Great Shepherd, shows us that balance. Time and time again, in Scripture, it says He went away alone to be with the Father.[27] He went away and said, "I've got to spend time here, with God, so that I can recharge to spend time there, with the people." In John, chapter 17, His entire prayer was: "You and I are one, Father." That has to be the baseline for the ministry of the pastor.

Pastor after pastor after pastor of churches have lost their family and their ministry because of "over-pastoring," because of burning out, because of "burning the candle at both ends," because of not realizing, "I don't need to be good

---

[27] Mark 1:35, for example.

for two years...I need to be good for 70 years, and therefore I've got to pace it. I've got to think about it. I've got to have my family with me. I don't want to lose my family."

It's edifying to minister with pastoral gifts, but don't let that edification replace your family. It can feel good to be used by God, but make sure your need to feel good by being used by God is not what's driving you to pastor other people.

    6. Pastors, recognize that you are talking with people who are in a time of need.

They have a need. They're drawing you into it. Often it's an emotional time. Be careful of your emotional involvement with the situation, and especially your emotional involvement with someone of the opposite sex. Many pastors—you hear it in the news on a regular basis, I know some of them personally—get involved in fornication, get involved in adultery, because they don't ensure a proper emotional distance.

I can feel compassion for you, but I don't have to be drawn into you, personally. We see this a lot in the church. People who are in need *need* someone to pay attention to them. The devil loves to open the door to improper relationships, improper sexual conduct, under the guise of counseling and helping someone. I believe that counseling is the devil's playground.

Many pastors fall by not recognizing they're becoming emotionally involved with a person. My advice to pastors is, never meet alone with a person of the opposite sex. I have asked my staff: Don't be in a car with someone of the opposite sex, that's not your spouse. Don't go out to eat for a lunch meeting with someone of the opposite sex, that's not your spouse. Don't do it alone. Why not? Because the father of lies has at least 6,000 years of experience turning compassionate emotions into lust and deceit and drawing people into darkness.

Another Look at Shepherds

The Old Testament prophet, Ezekiel, had a divine word for shepherds. In chapter 34, verses one through six, it's recorded:

> "Then the word of the Lord came to me saying, 'son of man, **prophesy against the shepherds of Israel.** Prophesy and say to those shepherds, "Thus says the Lord God, **'Woe to the shepherds of Israel who have been feeding themselves!** Should not the shepherds feed the flock? You eat the fat and clothe yourselves with the wool, you slaughter the fat sheep without feeding the flock. Those who are sickly you have not strengthened, the diseased you have not healed, the broken you have not bound up, the scattered you have not brought back, nor have you sought for the lost; but with force and with severity you have dominated them. They were scattered for lack of a shepherd, and they became food for every beast of the field and were scattered. My flock wandered through all the mountains and on every high hill; My flock was scattered over all the surface of the earth, and **there was no one to search or seek for them.'"'"**

What a great way to end the message on being a pastor! It sounds very condemning; it sounds very convicting. The first time I read this passage, I thought, "I don't want to use this Scripture. It just seems to be beating everybody up." But then the Holy Spirit said, "You're missing the job description, aren't you?" The Lord was saying, "This is what My shepherds should have been doing, and they were not."

In other words, would you like a list of what shepherds should be doing? Here it is. If you feel like that call is for you, to be a shepherd in this flock, I want you to notice the job description that He lays out here.

The Lord says, through Ezekiel, "Woe to the shepherds of Israel who have been feeding themselves! Should not the shepherds feed the flock?"

- Feeding the flock.

Your ministry is to ensure that the people of this flock get fed with the *logos* and *rhema* words of God. Drive them back to Scripture. Drive them back to hearing from the Lord. Don't worry about feeding yourself; worry that the people are getting fed.

- "You eat the fat and clothe yourselves with wool. You slaughter the fat sheep without feeding the flock."

Here's what I was saying above: Pastors can get caught up in meeting their own need to pastor. "I feel good when I'm helping someone else." "I feel God smiling at me when I'm helping someone else." "I just want to help more people so that I feel better." "I'm actually pastoring for my own benefit, not for their benefit." "I'm meeting my own needs by pastoring; I'm getting my own desires to feel approved by God in what I'm doing, instead of my focus being, 'How do I help them?'"

- "Those who are sickly you have not strengthened."

Pastors, stand beside the weak. Stand with them. Be there with them. Minister to the weak who need to be strengthened.

- "The diseased you have not healed,..."

Pray for those who need physical healing. Believe in that healing. Let them be healed by Jesus Christ, our Savior.

- "The broken you have not bound up,..."

This is a big deal at Revive Church. We're not talking about broken bones; we're talking about the broken soul. We're talking about the pains and the hurts of your past. We're talking about your unforgiveness. We're talking about your resentment. We're talking about your anxiety. We're talking about those things that contributed to you being busted up.

We have an inner healing ministry in this church. We have opportunities to say, "Let's go in and bind up what's been broken. Let's pull it back together. Let's care for those people. Let's drive them back to the Savior, drive them to the Holy Spirit, and let's bind up what's broken in them."

- "The scattered you have not brought back,..."

Those who feel rejected and outcast by the church would be "the scattered." I hear this phrase on a regular basis: "I have church hurt." No, you don't. You have hurt because someone in the church hurt you. Do not apply your church to the hurt; apply it to the person who has hurt you; and, let's talk about forgiveness so that you can move on.

Here's what I'm saying: If you don't deal with that woundedness, then what you do is you go to the next church, and you see it through the bias of that past wound. You're expecting to get hurt again, like you were hurt before. You never get healed to recognize that there was someone there with bad doctrine; there was someone with bad theology; there was someone who was autocratic; there was someone, who didn't understand, who hurt you. I agree—that may be absolutely true, but you don't have to carry it. That's baggage you don't have to keep carrying.

- "Nor have you sought the lost;..."

Seeking the lost, for me, means that a shepherd is always saying, "You need the Great Shepherd. You need to be healed eternally by Jesus."

- "But with force and severity you have dominated them."

Do you remember when Peter said, "I want you to serve with eagerness. I want you to have a humility that God designed you to do this and not expect a following because of how good you are with people"?

- "They were scattered for lack of a shepherd,..."

I think this is probably the most important thing that our shepherds need to be aware of today, in the church, because the enemy is striving hard to divide the church. It is the shepherds who must say, "No, the flock must stay together. I will not put up with disunity. I will not put up with sarcastic comments about leaders. I will not put up with bad doctrine slipping in. I will not put up with people deciding they have to leave this church and go start another one, because that's disunity in the body. I want the flock together. I want their strength to be in their numbers. I want them to follow the Great Shepherd."

Your Commission

Shepherds, pastors, you are herdsmen. You help the flock. You protect the flock. You keep the flock together. You ensure that the flock is hearing from the Great Shepherd.

FIVEFOLD FRAMEWORK

We need you. You're the glue. You're the bonding agent. You are the ones that walk us through the tough times. You have an obvious role in the health of the entire body. You are uniquely designed to minister to people who are in need. Pastors can bring together an incredible unity in the body.

If I'm speaking to you, if you're hearing that call, if you're recognizing, "I'm that way! I'm always thinking, 'This person's hurting. I need to talk to them...'" Or, "What are we going to do about this?" Or, "I just feel like I'm stressed, because I know they're struggling and I just want to step in..." If that's you, we need you here. We need you to minister to the flock. We need you to help us stay together. We need your words of encouragement.

I am 62 years old. I think I was born in a church service, meaning, I don't know what day of the week I was actually born on—I can go figure that out—but, I'll promise you, whatever the next church service was, my family took me to church. I was raised in church. I've been in churches, in different denominations, for all of my life. I have 62 years of experience at being in churches.

In all of that time, I have never met anyone who more conforms to the description of a pastor in Scripture than the one I'm going to ask to close this chapter. This is an individual who *knows* how to connect, who knows *when* to connect, who knows *what to say* when he connects with a person. This is someone who knows *how* to pastor, who cares about the body, who wants to bring them together. That person is Mr. Rick Evans.

Draw Near to God[28]

Revive Church has multiple pastors. I would venture to guess that Pastor Todd nailed it at 50 plus; it could be 80 or a hundred. Many of you know who you are.

I got saved, gave my life to Christ, when I was 16 years old, and days after I gave my life to Christ, I was walking the halls of Martin County High School and I noticed that things were different. I saw people differently. As I grew in my faith, I felt the need almost immediately to rescue people. This proves that God will take selfish individuals, like me, and turn them all around so that they feel the need to rescue people.

Everything Pastor Todd said is true. Everything about all the things that pastors are tempted to be and how we're motivated, it's all true. Here is the key to unravel and unfold who you are, and what are you're supposed to do in the ministry: "Draw near to God and He will draw near to you."[29]

Seek God with all your heart and He will come to you and He will walk you through. He will unravel for you and unfold for you what He has.

If you think you may be a pastor, don't go online and try to take a course on how to be a pastor. Don't try to go to school to study about it. Moses couldn't do that. David didn't do that. Instead, they connected with our heavenly Father. Jesus only did what He heard the Father telling Him to do.[30]

---

[28] This portion of the message provided by Rick Evans, Director of Pastoral Care at Revive Church.

[29] James 4:8

[30] John 8:28-29

FIVEFOLD FRAMEWORK

I encourage you to draw near to God today and He'll draw near to you. Seek Him with all your heart. Let's pray.

Father, thank You, Lord, for what You're doing right now. Father, I want to weep as You're pouring out Your Holy Spirit on a generation, Lord, on many generations right now. You're calling us to Your side and You're calling us to serve Your kingdom and Your purposes, because that is where our joy is found. That is where our purpose is found, and that is who we are in Christ.

I pray now, Lord, in Jesus' name, that everyone reading this book would surrender their hearts to You, would come before You and say, "I give up. I give in. I surrender to You, Lord."

I pray now, in Jesus' name, that You would give people boldness and courage to get on their knees and seek You with all their heart, that we would stop going our own direction and stop making our own decisions and stop doing our own thing and surrender our lives to You.

Thank You, Father, for what's happening in these hearts. Thank You for the many people who are coming to Christ today. Thank You for people who are surrendering their entire lives to You. It's in Jesus' name we pray, Amen.

RESURRECTING PASTORS

FIVEFOLD FRAMEWORK

RESURRECTING TEACHERS

In this book, we have been discussing resurrecting what's known as "the fivefold ministry." This refers to the five ministries that Christ gave to the church so that His body can be fully functional on earth. In examining these at length, we want to also discover what *your* particular ministry is: What is He working in you? So far, we have talked about apostles, prophets, evangelists and pastors. In this chapter, we're going to talk about the ministry of the teacher.[31]

Our base Scripture for this discussion comes from the Apostle Paul's letter to the Ephesians, chapter four, verses 11-13:

> **"And He [Christ] gave some as apostles, and some as prophets, and some as evangelists, and some as pastors and teachers**, for the equipping of the saints for the work of service, to the building up of the body of Christ; until we all attain to the unity of the faith and of the knowledge of the Son of God, to a mature man, to the measure of the stature which belongs to the fullness of Christ."

---

[31] Based on the message, "Resurrecting Teachers," September 1, 2024. https://reviveusnow.com/watch

The Ministry of the Teacher

If we break down what teaching is, in its simplest form, we all recognize that teaching generally amounts to explaining information and transferring knowledge others. That's what teaching is; that's what a teacher does. We look to teachers to explain information to us so that we can grow in knowledge.

In Ephesians, chapter four, however, the Greek word that's used for "teacher" actually has an extended meaning. The way the word "teacher" is used here, it is referring to those who "in the religious assemblies of Christians undertake the work of a teacher with the special assistance of the Holy Spirit." As the word is used in this instance, teaching is not just the transfer of knowledge, it's the transfer of knowledge "in the assembly of the Christian, with the assistance of the Holy Spirit."

This is what sets the ministry of the teacher apart from every other teacher on the planet. Every other teacher is not explaining the Scriptures of God with the assistance of the Holy Spirit. The ministry of the teacher carries the responsibility of explaining Scripture, not just any information, with the assistance of the Holy Spirit.

If you're operating in the ministry of the teacher, you're going to *need* the power of the Holy Spirit! We're talking about teaching 66 books worth of material, set out in 1,189 chapters, 31,102 verses and 782,815 words. Ready? Go! That's a lot of information.

Yet, Paul tells us in his second letter to Timothy, chapter three, verses 16 and 17, that

> **"All Scripture is inspired by God and profitable for teaching**, for reproof, for correction, for training in righteousness; so that

the man of God may be adequate, equipped for every good work."

If you are going to tell me that you want to teach the Scriptures *without* the assistance of the Holy Spirit, I would not want to learn from you.

The Work of the Holy Spirit

Jesus made it clear that to understand spiritual things, we are going to need help from the Holy Spirit. He told His disciples, in the Gospel of John, chapter 16, verses 12-15,

> *"I have many more things to say to you, but you cannot bear them now.* ***But when He, the Spirit of truth* [the Holy Spirit]*, comes, He will guide you into all the truth;*** *for He will not speak on His own initiative, but whatever He hears, He will speak; and He will disclose to you what is to come. He will glorify Me, for He will take of Mine and will disclose it to you. All things that the Father has are Mine; therefore I said that He takes of Mine and will disclose it to you."*

Revelation of the Scripture comes from whom? It comes from the Holy Spirit. The Holy Spirit – the Spirit of truth - gives us revelation of the Scripture.

Was Jesus speaking about something new? Not really. If we go back to Old Testament days, we see that God planned to reveal knowledge and give in-the-moment guidance to Moses when he went before Pharoah in Egypt.

The story, from the Book of Exodus, tells how God spoke to Moses from the burning bush and gave him the mission of asking for the release of the Hebrew captives who had been serving the Egyptian Pharoah for years. Moses is very reluctant to approach Pharoah with this request. From Exodus, chapter four, verses 10-12,

> Then Moses said to the Lord, "Please, Lord, I have never been eloquent, neither recently nor in time past, nor since You have spoken to Your servant; for I am slow of speech and slow of tongue." The Lord said to him, "Who has made man's mouth? Or who makes him mute or deaf, or seeing or blind? Is it not I, the Lord? **Now then go, and I, even I, will be with your mouth, and teach you what you are to say."**

Here's my point: The first mention of teaching in the Bible is God speaking to Moses. "The Rule of First Mention" says that, wherever a word or concept is first mentioned in Scripture, that becomes your basis for understanding that word or concept. Here, God is saying, "*I will teach you. You will speak what I teach you to speak.*" All Moses has to do is keep listening to God; God will teach him what to say.

In the same way, today, the ministry of the teacher involves listening to God. The Spirit of truth takes spiritual things from God and delivers them to the teacher. When the Holy Spirit "searches the deep things of God," then He can release them to us,[32] for everything that we have to learn is already known by God.

A Great Responsibility

Since everything that we could possibly ever learn in our lifetime is already known by God, a teacher's capacity to

---

[32] 1 Corinthians 2:10

learn is limited by his willingness to hear from God. God has all knowledge! The Holy Spirit's work is to disclose it to us. One thing that's going to severely limit our teaching capacity is not wanting to hear what He has to say.

In turn, the teacher's capacity to teach could be further limited by a lack of desire to take what God has given him and transfer it to others. The ability to teach can be limited if a teacher chooses to hear from God but then chooses to not deliver that message.

Therefore, teachers bear a great responsibility in Scripture. Not only do they need to listen to the Holy Spirit, but they need to be willing to deliver the Spirit's revelations to the church. Others may or may not understand spiritual things based on the teachers that are listening to the Holy Spirit in the church.

It makes sense, then, that the ministry of the teacher comes with a warning. Let's look at the letter that the Apostle James wrote, in chapter three, verses one through five, for that warning:

> **"Let not many of you become teachers, my brethren, knowing that as such we will incur a stricter judgment.** For we all stumble in many ways. If anyone does not stumble in what he says, he is a perfect man, able to bridle the whole body as well. Now if we put a bit into the horses' mouths so that they will obey us, we direct their entire body as well. Look at the ships also, though they are so great and are driven by strong winds, are still directed by a very small rudder wherever the inclination of the pilot desires. So also the tongue is a small

part of the body, and yet it boasts of great things."

What did he just say is the warning given to teachers? If you teach, you are one person affecting many people. One person, a teacher, can affect the direction of an entire expression of the body of Christ. Therefore, he says, "Let not many of you become teachers because you'll incur a stricter judgment, because what you say will affect the body and the body will follow."

Teaching is a huge responsibility and James here warns the teachers that they will be accountable for what they teach the body of Christ.

Are Teachers Perfect?

When James said that if any teacher doesn't stumble in his words he is "a perfect man," does that mean that teachers are perfect when they teach? No. If a person working in the ministry of the teacher is listening to the Holy Spirit, then many truths can be revealed. But, if they do not listen to the Holy Spirit, then the flesh gets involved and the result is false teaching.

Jesus' warning against false teachers is recorded in the Gospel of Matthew, chapter 15, verses seven to fourteen. He's talking to the Pharisees:

"You hypocrites, rightly did Isaiah prophesy of you:

'THIS PEOPLE HONORS ME WITH THEIR LIPS,
BUT THEIR HEART IS FAR AWAY FROM ME.
'BUT IN VAIN DO THEY WORSHIP ME,
TEACHING AS DOCTRINES THE PRECEPTS OF MEN.'"

After Jesus called the crowd to Him, He said to them, *"Hear and understand. It is not what enters*

> *into the mouth that defiles the man, but what precedes out of the mouth, this defiles the man."*
>
> Then the disciples came and said to Him, "Do you know that the Pharisees were offended when they heard this statement?" But He answered and said, *"Every plant which My heavenly Father did not plant shall be uprooted. Let them alone;* **they are blind guides of the blind. And if a blind man guides a blind man, both will fall into a pit."**

A "blind" teacher, one who is not led by the Spirit, one who is teaching the precepts of men as doctrine, leads people into darkness. Don't miss the fact that Jesus said, not only does that teacher fall into the pit, but the student falls into the pit along with the teacher.

The Apostle Peter also refers to false teachers in his second letter, chapter two, verses one through three:

> "But false prophets also arose among the people, just as **there will also be false teachers among you, who will secretly introduce destructive heresies, even denying the Master who bought them, bringing swift destruction upon themselves.** Many will follow their sensuality, and because of them the way of the truth will be maligned; and in their greed they will exploit you with false words; their judgment from long ago is not idle, and their destruction is not asleep."

One of the things we just learned from these two Scriptures is not only is there a responsibility of what you teach, but there's a responsibility for what you hear, what you learn.

Jesus said both teacher and student are going to fall into a pit, so the teacher needs to be responsible for what he is learning. He still has a responsibility as a listener.

When Paul and Silas were traveling on their missionary journey, they encountered some new believers that understood this responsibility. It's described in chapter 17 of the Book of the Acts of the Apostles, verses 10-11:

> The brethren [in Thessalonica] immediately sent Paul and Silas away by night to Berea, and when they arrived, they went into the synagogue of the Jews. Now these were more noble-minded than those in Thessalonica, **for they received the word with great eagerness, examining the Scriptures daily to see whether these things were so.**

This is the accountability of the listener saying, "I have to go back and confirm what I'm being taught before I believe in that." As believers, we have to investigate what we're being taught, because Peter tells us there will be false teachers.

For the Love of Teaching

With all of these warnings, all of these flashing red lights, all of these responsibilities, why would anybody want to be a teacher? I'll tell you why *I* do. It's because of a passage in the Gospel of Luke, chapter 24, verses 44-45.

Jesus is speaking to His disciples. He has already been resurrected. He is teaching them in a 40-day period, before He ascends into heaven.

> Now He [Jesus] said to them, *"These are my words which I spoke to you while I was still with you, that all things which are written about Me in*

FIVEFOLD FRAMEWORK

the Law of Moses and the Prophets and the Psalms must be fulfilled."

Jesus is saying, "You have been reading about the Law of Moses, the Prophets and the Psalms, and there's stuff in there about Me. Every bit of that has to be fulfilled."

Now, verse 45 is the one that turned the light on for me:

Then He [Jesus] opened their minds to understand the Scriptures,...

That one verse just *intrigued* me, because what I'm hearing Luke say is, they had been reading Scriptures the whole time, but never understanding the truth.

These were Jesus' disciples! These were the ones who had been waiting for the Messiah. But He said, "You've been reading this Scripture, but you've never understood it. What I'm going to do is, I'm going to 'open your mind' so that you can understand what it is you're reading."

What does that tell us? It tells us that we can actually read the Scripture without understanding. Have you ever read something and you're absolutely blind to what it actually says? I'm not that huge of a book-reader, because every time I get to the bottom of the page, I'm thinking, "I have no idea what that page just said… I was thinking about what I've got to do tomorrow… I read every word, but I have no idea what that just said." I think that's kind of a picture of what Jesus is saying here. You can read this stuff and have no clue about what you're reading.

That level of understanding is available to every believer, the Holy Spirit can open everyone's mind to understand the Scripture. Why? Because He is the Spirit of truth and He dwells in you. He *wants* you to understand.

Be aware, however, that if you're in the ministry of the teacher, that understanding from the Holy Spirit *has to be* present. That's the definition of a teacher in Ephesians, chapter four — that you're assisted by the Spirit. After all, why would the Lord give you a ministry to teach and then leave you without the inspiration of the Holy Spirit to try to figure the Scriptures out? That doesn't make sense.

The Spirit Opens the Scriptures

How many of us have sat under a teacher that explains the obvious? "Yeah, I just heard you tell that whole story. You said the same thing everybody says about that. You explained it the same way everybody else has. I learned nothing from that..." It's a whole different story when, under the inspiration of the Holy Spirit, someone takes a Scripture and opens it up to what it actually can mean and how it connects to other Scripture.

I'll give you an example. Four or five years ago, I was reading about Ruth and Boaz. If you have never read the Book of Ruth in the Old Testament, it's only four chapters. Go home and read it today. The story of Ruth and Boaz is actually the story of Jesus redeeming His people.

Ruth is the daughter-in-law of Naomi. First Naomi loses her husband, then Ruth also is widowed. In that culture, women had no means of making a living apart from men. The only hope for Ruth and Naomi is for them to be "redeemed," or taken into the care of someone from their husbands' family.

In the story, the man who was "next in line" to redeem them says he doesn't want to redeem them into his family. (By the way, the first man represents the Law.) The next man, Boaz,

FIVEFOLD FRAMEWORK

steps up and says, "I will redeem these two into my home. They'll become part of my family. I will redeem them."

The process of redeeming them involved going to the elders at the city gate, untying his shoe, taking it off and presenting it as what the Scripture says is an "attestation," a testimony that says, "This is true, what I'm doing. I am redeeming these women into my family. I've taken off my shoe."

Why taking your shoe off is the symbol, I don't know,... unless it's what I'm about to tell you: He takes his shoe off as an attestation that he was redeeming Ruth and Naomi. That was the testimony that he was providing redemption.

Now, you go to the New Testament, and in the days before Jesus began His ministry, the forerunner that we know as "John the Baptist" declares, "I am not the redeemer." Let's read it from the Gospel of John, chapter one, verses 19-20:

> This is the testimony of John when the Jews sent to him priests and Levites from Jerusalem to ask him, "Who are you?" **And he confessed and did not deny, but confessed, "I am not the Christ."**

Then further on, in verses 26-27, we read,

> John answered them saying, "I baptize in water, but among you stands One whom you do not know. **It is He who comes after me, the thong of whose sandal I am not worthy to untie."**

I've heard this Scripture taught over and over again. Everybody said, "Oh, this is about humility. This is about bowing down. This is about going to the groveling place."

But, actually, this is where John the Baptist says, "I am not the redeemer. I am not even worthy to untie his shoes." John was saying, "I can't do the attestation of redemption, because I'm not the savior. Jesus is. I can't even take off his shoe."

All of a sudden, you're looking at this Scripture and you're thinking, "Oh, you mean it wasn't about John going down near stinky feet and doing something really humble?" No, he was identifying attestation for redemption, that it belonged to Jesus, not to him.

It's a whole different thing when the Spirit starts opening your eyes to see deeper meanings in the Scriptures. You have to remember, though, as a teacher, you can take no credit for the revelation. The teacher doesn't generate the revelation. The Holy Spirit generates the revelation, because He wants something to be taught. There should be no ego or arrogance. The teacher seeks to be taught by the Holy Spirit so that he can impart knowledge to others, so he can share the revelation, so others can grow. That's how it works.

Are You Called to be a Teacher?

Are you operating in the ministry of a teacher? You might be a teacher if…

- Scripture is legitimately exciting for you. You want to go in there and dig stuff out. You want to see what it says.
- You see connections in the Bible that other people are not seeing. You believe the Holy Spirit is showing you hidden things that you're supposed to teach others.
- You feel like there's a lifetime of learning in those 66 books of the Bible. You don't read that thing once and say, "I got it."

I've been reading the Bible for over 40 years and I still don't "got it." I feel like I'm just pecking at the surface, because every time God shows me something a little better, I'm thinking, "There's more; there's more in there; I've got to get to the more."

- You desire to read the Bible just to find out what you don't know. You want to read the Bible because there are things you don't know and you want to understand them; you know they're in there.
- You want others to see what you have been shown in Scripture, and it comes naturally to you as to how to roll out that revelation to others.

What do I mean by that? Teachers are assisted by the Holy Spirit as to how to explain the revelation. It will come fairly naturally. As they prepare a message, they'll be thinking, "Oh yeah, I've got to lay the foundation; I've got to talk about this; I've got to go here. I can't go here, because that will be a 'rabbit trail,' I need to stay here, and then, they'll get to here." All of that becomes very natural for a teacher.

- Things hit you in the Spirit when other people teach.

You're listening to somebody teach and you say, "Oh, that was good, that was good." Or, you're thinking, "Ooh, ooh, where did he get *that*? That doesn't make sense. How can that be true, if this is true over here?" A teacher will be analyzing, with the Holy Spirit, what's being taught.

- You get frustrated when you hear wrong things being taught.

There's a lesson to learn in that because sometimes you just don't know yet. Sometimes, I've heard teachers teach things and what hit me in my spirit was not, "That's wrong," but, "I don't understand that, but that might be worth looking into. I don't get it today; that doesn't work for me; but, that sounded solid. I want to go research that."

- Finally, you might be a teacher if you are scared to death to teach something wrong.

If you know you're going to get hit with the emails on Monday and you're going to have to apologize next Sunday. This makes you really look it over and ask yourself, "Is this solid? Is this Biblically foundational? Can I teach this? I want to get it right. I'm going to be affecting the whole body."

Too many teachers in the church at large today have lost the fear of God in their teaching. They've lost the understanding of the responsibility of what they say. There are so many false teachers out there today. Why? Why did he warn us there would be false teachers? Why are they out there? We just read it in Second Peter, chapter two, verse two:

> "Many will follow their sensuality, and because of them the way of the truth will be maligned; and in their greed they will exploit you with false words;…"

What is the thing Peter said that drives false teachers? Teaching "sensuality," meaning, teaching what appeals to people. "What do people want to hear? What makes them happy to come and hear me? What leaves them thinking, 'Oh, that was so good! I feel so much better'?" That's called teaching sensuality. The Scripture sometimes calls it, "tickling their ears."[33]

An example of a false teaching is teaching "prosperity" without teaching "holiness." Another one, related to that, is teaching "reward" without teaching "sacrifice." Scripture

---

[33] 2 Timothy 4:3

also says these teachers can be greedy, wanting fame or income based on their teaching.

A Smattering of False Teachings

I want to talk about some relevant false teachings that are out there in the church at large. These are things that I hear being taught, that I know are not from the Holy Spirit.

- "God needs our permission to do anything on this earth."

Some people say that God gave mankind dominion here on earth; we gave it up to Satan; Christ gave it back to us; now we have dominion on the earth again, so what happens on the earth is up to us. God will then need to ask us if He wants to do anything on the earth. By the way, they also teach that God is waiting for us to give Him permission to do things on the earth. If we just give Him permission, then He would fix everything.

That teaching is garbage. If someone *gives* you authority, they *have* authority over you. How could they give you authority if they don't have authority over you to give you the authority? It makes no sense. That would put *us* in charge of God.

- "Once we are saved, we are free to sin because we are eternally forgiven."

They call that "free grace." "God loves you so much that He will always forgive you. You're free to sin; it's okay. It's not going to be held against you because you have Jesus and His blood."

If you believe that, you do not understand what Christ did for you. You don't understand what He did on the cross, and you don't understand what it means to be transferred from the kingdom of darkness into the kingdom of God. You don't understand that God is going to discipline His children for sin. I refer you to the Book of Hebrews, chapter 12, verse six,

> "FOR THOSE WHOM THE LORD LOVES HE DISCIPLINES, AND HE SCOURGES EVERY SON WHOM HE RECEIVES."

It's as if God says, "You are My son; now I will discipline you." Notice it doesn't say, "I'm going to 'put you in timeout.'" It says He "scourges." In other words, the ramification for my sin, the consequences for choosing to go back into the realm of darkness, can be very severe. If I knew not to do it, but I did it anyways, I'm not going to get a slap on the hand and told, "Let's go home..." I may go through years, struggling and dealing with something, because I submitted to the enemy when I sinned.

- "The Bible, in its earliest text, originally condoned homosexuality, but it was retranslated around 600 AD to speak against it."

This false teaching says that the Bible originally said homosexuality was okay, but then they retranslated it around 600 AD to say that now, it's not okay. That's the only reason why the church gets all upset, because they think it's not okay, when in the original text, it was okay...

But, we still *have* the original text! Not the original, because it doesn't exist, but we've got stuff going way back before 600 AD. We've got stuff going back into hundreds and hundreds of years before Christ that confirm what the Scripture said.

If you believe that God is okay with homosexuality, then you don't understand the character of God; you don't understand the "marriage of the Lamb," of the Groom to the Bride of Christ; you don't understand "filling the earth:" reproduction; you don't understand, naturally, what we were supposed to do; you don't understand a man "leaving his father and mother to cling to a wife;" or, you don't understand the depraved mind mentioned in Paul's letter to the Romans, chapter one.[34]

I read that in my own child's college textbook, that God was okay with homosexuality until 600 AD, when the translators rewrote the versions so that He condemned it. Unbelievable.

- "God cares most about you being happy."

This is the "God is all about me" theology. What it does is, it reduces God to a good buddy and a happy-feelings fairy; instead of, the Creator of the universe: righteous, mighty, just, holy and judging; who can squash you like a bug.

It was never about us! It was about Him and what He wanted to do. All glory, all honor, all go to Him. Without Him, I'm not even here! I can be taken out right now by Him.

- "Jesus is tolerant of all sin because He's loving."

This is running rampant right now in the church. "He is tolerant of all sin because He's loving. And if you were loving, you would just be tolerant of sin." Then, why did Jesus call out the sin in people and tell them to stop? Why was the message, "Repent from your sin and believe on Jesus Christ"?[35]

When Jesus ate with tax collectors, it does not mean that He approved of corruption and greed. When He sat with the prostitute, it does not mean that He paid her for her time. When you are caught in adultery by Jesus, He will tell you,

---

[34] Revelation 19 / Genesis 1-2 / Romans 1

[35] Acts 2:22-40

"Go, but sin no more." Jesus is saying, "I will die for you, but it's not okay for you to stay in your sin. You're in the kingdom of God, now that darkness should be behind you."

Further Warnings

Besides the danger of falling into false teachings, I have four warnings for people who take on the ministry of the teacher.

- Take the teaching responsibility seriously.

God has told us you will be under a stricter judgment. If you just want to be a teacher who teaches new, shiny things and surprising Scriptural mysteries, I promise you, you will get into trouble. I promise you, it'll lead you into error.

You can learn or see something and not discuss it with the Holy Spirit and end up being a false teacher. Don't go digging in Scripture with the purpose of trying to find something that no one else knows, that no one's ever seen before. "I want a new, revealed, hidden mystery." Why not? You're asking for trouble. You're asking for the enemy to lead you astray.

Here's what you do: You go into the Scripture to study the Scripture and you let the Holy Spirit take you to things you did not know. That's where revelation comes from, not because I'm going in and saying, "I want to teach something that no one's ever taught before me. Show me something cool." The Holy Spirit says, "Come back when you're serious."

- Don't fall into the trap of hearing what someone else taught and thinking it's right to teach.

There are plenty of big-name teachers who have had to repent of what they taught. Some will teach just the traditional, safe, easy view, because it's all they know. Some will teach "crazy," because they want attention for what they teach. Many will latch onto the latest craze. "I'll just join the bandwagon and teach what everybody else is teaching." Some will just flat get it wrong because they're not listening to the Spirit. Some will teach you their denomination's pet doctrines.

If you're ever in my office, behind my desk, there are some degrees on the wall. There's a degree from Temple Baptist Seminary, where I went through years of seminary training to find out that "the gifts don't exist anymore," and that "the fivefold ministry doesn't exist anymore." You can be taught a "denomination," meaning, a certain denomination's beliefs, and not be taught the truth. After being baptized in the Holy Spirit, I had to unlearn a lot of what I learned in seminary.

I'm not saying that we cannot be taught by other teachers. I'm saying, if you are going to teach the Bible, teach what the Holy Spirit gives you to teach, not what some other man or woman gives you to teach. Teach what the Holy Spirit gives *you* to teach. If you cannot become completely convinced of it, Scripturally, don't teach it. If you do not get confirmation from the Holy Spirit on what you're learning, don't teach it. If you don't feel like you completely understand the topic you're teaching, don't teach it.

Don't teach something before it's time to teach it. See, you're getting that revelation for a reason. You're getting intrigued and convicted to go further for a reason. If you get ahead of that reason, you will teach something before it's time to teach it. Most of the time, you'll wish you hadn't taught it, because of what you learned later. Don't be in a hurry to teach. Let it simmer, pray on it. Spend time with the Spirit asking, "Is this what You want me to release?"

- Teaching is not a ticket to popularity.

YouTube has created a market for false teachers. These teachers are looking for "likes" and subscriptions and an income from their living room studios. Most of them are teaching someone else's messages, just in order to have content for their site.

Have you ever seen this? Have you ever seen the reels that come through, if you're a Facebook fan, where somebody's showing you this really cool thing that they found in Genesis, chapter one? Then, you scroll a little further and here's another person saying, "Oh, look what the Spirit showed me in Genesis, chapter one!" And then, you go a little further and there's another reel and it's somebody sitting at a desk with their Bible open: "I'm going to teach you today from Genesis, chapter one..." and they all teach the exact same thing! Why? Because they're listening to each other. They're not getting their information from the Spirit; they're getting it from Facebook and other YouTubers. They just want to regurgitate something that they think people would be interested in.

Teaching over YouTube can still be done very, very, very well. It's just that many of those teachers are false teachers just trying to draw an audience or an income. Some people just need affirmation, so they use teaching on a public social media platform to get affirmations. "Oh, look how many likes I've got. Look how many subscribers I have..."

- The *rhema* Word of God will never contradict the *logos* Word of God.

What does that mean? When you go into the Greek, in the New Testament, and you see the word, "word," it's actually two different Greek words that have different meanings. When you see the word "word" in Scripture, you have to

FIVEFOLD FRAMEWORK

know, is it translated from *logos* or from *rhema*? What's the difference? Both of those get translated as "word."

A *"logos* word" means anything that's already established, written or decreed. In other words, when I look at the Old Testament prophets, and the New Testament writers are quoting them, they are quoting the *logos* word. They are saying, "Does it not say in the Book of Isaiah that 'by His stripes we were healed'?" They are quoting a *logos* word, something already written or established.

A *"rhema* word" is the currently spoken word, as in, "somebody had a word for me today; they said something to me today." Here's an example in Scripture: Christ is in the desert. Satan is there saying, "Why don't you take these rocks and turn them into bread?" Christ says, "Man doesn't live by bread alone, but he lives by every word..." Oh, guess what? He used *rhema*. "...he lives by every *rhema* word that proceeds..." (not that proceeded) "... that proceeds out of the mouth of God." What is Jesus saying? "I live by the Spirit. I am hearing from God on a daily basis. I don't need bread. If I'm supposed to fast, I will fast."[36]

There are two different types of words given, but that *rhema* word that you get in a dream, that you get from someone else, that you hear spoken to you, will never contradict what is already said and established by God, the *logos* word. God doesn't change His mind or change His doctrines or change His theology or say, "Oh wait, I've got something new for you that's different from what I told you before." When someone says, "I've got a word today that God wants you to divorce your husband,..." that's not from God. That would

---

[36] Matthew 4:1-4

contradict the God whose *logos* word says, "I hate divorce."[37] (If you're divorced, don't sweat. We can talk about that, too.)

The word that's released, the *rhema* word, will not contradict Scripture, the *logos* word. They are always consistent. Often an immature teacher is so hungry for revelation that they will take whatever they hear and not realize it's coming from a spirit, but not the Holy Spirit. So when you hear something, you have to go back to God's word and ask, "Is this consistent with the character of God?"

As an example, I heard a teacher who "listened to the Spirit," it just wasn't the Holy Spirit, that got them off the track in such a way that it sounded like it made sense, but it didn't. It was wrong and it was false. This was a woman teaching. She said, "If Jesus were giving the Sermon on the Mount today, He might add, 'Blessed are those who end pregnancies for they will be known for their lovingkindness.'"

How do you take the *logos* word that says shedding innocent blood is wrong[38] and say, by a *rhema* word, presumably, that Jesus would now say it's okay? This is taking the Word and skewing it to try to touch you emotionally. It's a bogus, false teaching.

(Now, if you've had an abortion, there is complete restoration and forgiveness for you. You serve a loving God. Don't ever think that God has turned His back on you. If you realize that abortion is shedding the blood of the innocent and is murder, don't ever turn your back on God. He is still running to you,

---

[37] Malachi 2:16

[38] Proverbs 6:17; Deuteronomy 19:10

hugging you, holding you, walking you through that saying, "Let's go forward.")

I believe Jesus' response, if this woman were willing to hear it, would be to grab her and hug her and say, "I love you. This was wrong. Don't do it again. Let's move forward."

A Few Reminders for Teachers

I have a few quick reminders for teachers.

1. Never approach Scripture without first asking the Holy Spirit to reveal to you what it means.

This is an important rule for every believer, but if you're a teacher, it's especially important for you. You may have the full revelation or you may not, but make sure it's the Holy Spirit giving you that revelation. Never go to the Scripture on your own and try to figure it out. Go to the Scripture with the Spirit and say, "Please show me what this means. Show me the connection. Show me how it works in the Kingdom."

2. A good Holy Spirit-driven teacher does not need gimmicks.

They don't need to fill the stage with water so they can talk about walking on the water. They don't need a sports car on the stage. They don't need to pour syrup over everything. They don't need gimmicks. Why not? Because the Word of God, in and of itself, has the authority and the power and the conviction to change lives, without toys.

Maybe, if what you're doing with the gimmicks is that important to you, you're more concerned about the show than you are about the Word? I'm not saying that demonstration and practical visuals are bad, that's not what I'm saying. But I am saying that, in many cases, it's gotten out of hand. It's possible for the people to remember what happened on the stage, but not remember the message.

3. Do not "cherry-pick" Scriptures out of context.

Facebook is king on this one—taking a Scripture out of its context, throwing condemnation on everybody, or throwing a grace on everybody that's not there. Taking a Scripture out of context means the Holy Spirit didn't guide you to the explanation of that Scripture.

For example, in the Gospel of Matthew, chapter 18, verses 19-20, Jesus says this to His disciples:

> *"Again I say to you, that if two of you agree on earth about anything that they may ask, it shall be done for them by My Father who is in heaven.* **For where two or three have gathered together in My name, I am there in their midst.**"

Have you ever heard this quoted? Have you ever heard it when you go to church? Have you ever heard it when you're in a prayer group? Have you ever heard it when you're in a small group? "Hey, two or three are here, so Jesus is in our midst."

Let's think that through: So, when you're by yourself, Jesus can't be in your midst? If I want to spend some time with Jesus, I need to get two or three people together so that He would "be in our midst"? He's not "in our midst" unless there are two or three together?

What is this Scripture talking about? It's talking about when a brother sins, we are to go to him privately, one on one, and convince him that he needs to repent. If he doesn't repent, we are to take two or three others with us and Jesus will "be in our midst."

I want you to consider why this makes sense: You have tried to do the Christian brotherly thing, by going to your brother privately; but, the Christian brotherly thing didn't work. So you take two or three others with you. What does the confronted person feel? "You're ganging up on me." No, Jesus says, "When two or three are gathered in My name, I will be in their midst," to make sure he has the opportunity to actually repent and receive what you're saying.

Jesus wants him to repent more than you do. He says, "If you'll do it this way, I'll go." Why? Because the next step is to take it to the church for church discipline. In other words, this is that person's last opportunity. "I will go with you if you'll do it with two or three. So there's no question about what was said, let's do it together, as a team. I'll be there with you. Pray we get this person to repent." It doesn't mean, "You can start the worship set now, because Jesus has arrived, since the second person came in the room…"

We Need Your Zeal

Teachers, we need you! We need Holy Spirit-inspired teaching. We need your zeal for the Word of God. You have a zeal for the Word that's not in everyone else. You have a desire to go in and dig it out. You have a desire to understand God's word that few others have.

We all have desires, but you have been given the ministry to have that desire to be assisted by the Spirit, to go in and get that revelation. We need your research. We need your prayer concerning Scripture. We need to know that you are teaching because you are being assisted by the Holy Spirit to explain it to us.

Without Spirit-led teachers, we can be deceived. Without Spirit-led teachers, we can have false teaching. Without Spirit-led teachers, we can wander in darkness as a body, with no one to direct or guide us. Without Spirit-led teachers, we will not fully know who we are in Christ. Without Spirit-led teachers, we don't understand the full gospel of Jesus Christ. Without Spirit-led teachers, we will not know how to abide in God, how to abide in Jesus, how to abide with the Holy Spirit.

Holy Spirit-led teachers are essential to the body of Christ. They are the bit, they are the rudder, and they must lead us in a holy and righteous direction when it comes to understanding the Word of God.

We've talked about apostles, we've talked about prophets, we've talked about evangelists, we've talked about pastors, we've talked about teachers. I'm praying that somewhere, in the midst of these chapters, one of those has connected with you. I've already had people come to me and say, "This makes sense. Now I know why I'm like I am. Now I see that this is a ministry that Christ has given me."

If this chapter on the ministry of the teacher has touched you, if you felt like, "That's me, that's me. When it comes to approaching Scripture, and understanding it, and getting those revelations, that's me. I don't always know what to do with it, but I am getting revelation and I'd like to explore that," I'd like you to find a trusted prayer minister to pray with you. If you are thinking, "I think that's me. I think I was meant to be working in the ministry of the teacher," please have someone pray with you to confirm it.

FIVEFOLD FRAMEWORK

Father God, in the name of Jesus, we are here because we want to hear from You, Holy Spirit, about the deep things of God. We want revelation. We want understanding. We want to move forward as the body of Christ.

For those God in this house that You're calling to teach, give them a peace that You will guide them through that process. Give them the patience to recognize they've got to hear from You and know when it's You and when it's not. Allow them to release Your word of the Scripture into this congregation.
In Jesus' name, Amen.

RESURRECTING UNITY

In our study of the fivefold ministry, we've covered each of the five ministries over the last five chapters. In this chapter, we will take this topic one step further and ask, "How do those five ministries work together in a church body?"[39]

We'll start with the Scripture we've begun with in each chapter—Paul's letter to the Ephesians, chapter four, verses 11-13:

> **"And He [Christ] gave some as apostles, and some as prophets, and some as evangelists, and some as pastors and teachers**, for the equipping of the saints for the work of service, to the building up of the body of Christ; until we all attain to the unity of the faith and of the knowledge of the Son of God, to a mature man, to the measure of the stature which belongs to the fullness of Christ."

As we've talked about the ministries that Christ gave to the church, hopefully, somewhere in the midst of that, you began to feel stirred. You began to say, "Wait a minute. He's describing *me*; I feel that way; I operate that way." "Maybe that's my opportunity? Maybe that's what God designed me

---

[39] Based on the message, "Resurrecting Unity in the 5 Fold Ministry," September 8, 2024. https://reviveusnow.com/watch

to do?" "I want to operate in the fullness of what God designed me to do."

If that's the case, we must now look at how you're going to do that. How are you going to operate in that ministry? How are you going to walk that out?

Operating in the Ministry

Fortunately, the Apostle Paul gives us some instructions, just before the passage we've been reading. At the beginning of Ephesians, chapter 4, verses 1-8, Paul says,

> "Therefore I, the prisoner of the Lord, implore you to walk in a manner worthy of **the calling with which you have been called,**..."

What is he talking about? He's referring to the fivefold ministry that he's about to explain. He says, "I want you to walk in a manner worthy of that calling — the one God has placed on you."

> "...with all humility and gentleness, with patience, showing tolerance for one another in love, being diligent to preserve the unity of the Spirit in the bond of peace. There is one body and one Spirit, just as also you were called in one hope of your calling; one Lord, one faith, one baptism, one God and Father over all who is through all and in all.
>
> **But to each one of us grace was given according to the measure of Christ's gift.** Therefore it says,
>
>> 'WHEN HE ASCENDED ON HIGH,
>> HE LED CAPTIVE A HOST OF CAPTIVES,
>> AND HE GAVE GIFTS TO MEN.'"

That's the reference to the gifts of the ministries: "He gave gifts to men."

Then Paul explains why he quotes from Psalm 68:18, about Christ ascending, in verses nine and ten, which is followed immediately by verses 11-13. This is the Scripture we've been studying: "He gave some as apostles, etc...." where the fivefold ministry is laid out.

We have spent a considerable amount of time, over the last five chapters, discussing the warning signs, traps and things that might get you off course when operating in your ministry. Ministries can be abused, poorly handled or diverted from their original intent. So Paul says, "If you're going to work in the ministry Christ gave you, do it well." Fortunately, he explains some of the key components of walking out your ministry well.

With All Humility

In verse two, Paul says, "When you walk your ministry out in a manner worthy of the calling to which you have been called, do it 'with all humility.'" Listen, I think the quickest way to be sidelined in the kingdom of God is to be prideful.

If you decide that you are very important because of what you're doing and what you "bring to the table," everything begins to go south. Because of your self-importance, your ministry will fail.

Do you know? God can replace you in a nanosecond! If you're going to make your ministry all about *you*, fine—God will find someone who can operate in humility and move on. You're not irreplaceable. Remember that; it's how you stay out of pride.

God designed you with distinct gifts and traits; therefore, let Him make a place for you; let Him set a path for you. He knows His design, why He gave a certain gift to you and He knows when and where and how He wants to use it. Let Him do it. Don't make decisions for God about how He's going to use the ministry He gave you in which to operate.

Gentleness and Patience

Paul advises us to operate "with all humility and gentleness, with patience." Let me tell you which two ministries are going to struggle the most with gentleness and patience: apostles and prophets.

Apostles and prophets don't have time to wait. "Things need to be done! Words need to be given, and words need to be obeyed. They need to move!" These ministries will struggle most with gentleness and patience. If you want to destroy your apostolic ministry or your prophetic ministry, be a jerk. Be a jerk, and it'll come to an end very quickly. Nobody wants to work with someone who's going to run over them like a Mack truck and then justify it by saying, "Well, this is the ministry God gave me."

But, guess which ministry is not going to struggle with gentleness and patience? Pastors. Pastors are *designed* to be patient, to "minister" to others, to care for people and to help them move forward.

Show Tolerance in Love

Next, Paul instructs us to show "tolerance for one another in love." Now, when we talk about tolerance, in general, we are talking about recognizing how people are designed differently, and accepting how people see other people and situations from different perspectives. But, stay within the context of what we're reading here: when he says, "showing tolerance for one another," he's not talking about tolerance for the members of the church body; he's talking about tolerance for other ministries. "Show love for one another as you each operate in various ministries. Show tolerance for one another in love."

This is when each ministry realizes how much it needs the other ministries. What do I mean by that? The Holy Spirit showed me that every ministry has a balancing ministry — another ministry that helps to balance it. Let me show you what I mean.

The Prophetic Ministry

The prophetic ministry is balanced by the pastoral ministry. Prophets often call for repentance, holiness, righteousness and doing things right in the sight of God. But here's the truth: that can absolutely wear believers out! When you're studying under someone who is prophetic, he is constantly call you to self-examination. He wants you to recognize sin and align yourself with God's righteousness.

The pastor balances the prophet, because the pastor says, "You're okay. You are striving to do the right thing, so don't be offended. Listen to what the prophet is saying — he's just trying to get us lined up with God. I'll walk with you through this self-examination; we all need correction from time to time..." So, the pastor takes the prophetic word and helps the people receive it.

The Ministry of the Evangelist

Let's look at the next one: the evangelist. The evangelist is balanced by the teacher. The evangelist's goal is to get people saved. They'll go anywhere and do anything, it seems, to lead someone to Christ. But once that person is saved, healed or delivered, where does the evangelist's mind go? "Who's next?" "Who else can I lead to Christ?" The teacher steps in to finish the job of discipleship. The teacher equips the new believer with the Word and their identity in Christ, helping him understand his authority in the kingdom of God. So, the teacher balances the evangelist by completing the process.

The Apostolic Ministry

Next, the apostolic ministry is balanced by the evangelistic ministry. The apostle focuses on structure, development, activation, handling groups of people and figuring out how to disciple them. The apostle can sometimes overlook the core reason for their ministry, because of the many responsibilities they juggle. The evangelist reminds the apostolic ministry that their purpose is rooted in salvation—leading people to Christ. Without the evangelist leading people to Christ, the apostolic ministry has no one to disciple or organize.

The Ministry of the Teacher

The teacher is balanced by the prophet. The teacher operates in the *logos*—the written Word of God, explaining Scripture to people. The prophet, on the other hand, operates in the *rhema*—the "now" Word of God. While the teacher gets revelation to explain the *logos*, the prophet receives words outside of Scripture. (As we mentioned in a previous chapter, the *rhema* Word must always align with Scripture, the *logos* Word.) Therefore, the Word and the Spirit come together through the teacher and prophet.

The Pastoral Ministry

Finally, the pastoral ministry is balanced by the apostolic ministry. Many pastors become frustrated because they can't meet everyone's needs. The apostolic ministry helps by organizing teams, building systems and creating discipleship programs, allowing pastors to focus on ministering to individuals.

This teamwork among the different callings of the fivefold ministry is crucial for moving the kingdom of God forward.

Being Diligent

Now, let's go back to how we are to use the ministries we've been given. In verse three of Ephesians, chapter four, Paul continues his instructions on how to "walk in a manner worthy of your calling," by saying, "…being diligent to preserve the unity of the Spirit in the bond of peace." People working together in the fivefold ministry must be diligent in preserving unity and peace.

The word "diligent" in Greek means "to exert oneself or endeavor to accomplish something." We must be intentional about preserving the oneness that the Holy Spirit offers, held together by the bond of peace. Peace is the bonding agent. So, the bottom line is, be intentional about maintaining peace and unity through the Holy Spirit.

Let's go back over the whole passage.

> "Therefore I, the prisoner of the Lord, implore you to walk in a manner worthy of the calling with which you have been called, **with all humility and gentleness, with patience, showing tolerance for one another in love,**

> **being diligent to preserve the unity of the Spirit in the bond of peace."**

That's how we're supposed to operate in ministry.

Oneness in the Lord

Now, the question is, why do we have to do that? Why is it so critical in the conversation? The answer is found in verses four through six:

> "There is **one body** and **one Spirit**, just as also you were called in **one hope** of your calling; **one Lord, one faith, one baptism, one God** and Father of all who is over all and through all and in all."

Are you seeing the repeated word there? "There is *one...*" Recognizing the oneness of who we are—our unity—is essential.

We will not find unity by agreeing with each other. We will agree with each other when we are in unity. What am I saying? We live in a world of compromise for agreement. When we have a disagreement, we say, "Let's talk about it until you give a little and I give a little, and then we find a middle ground where we can say we are in agreement." That is not unity; that is compromise.

Unity is when, because we are one, we come into agreement. Because we are one, we operate in agreement. Because we are one, we don't need to compromise. We know what the "one" is, and we make our decisions around the "one." We are in agreement because we are one. Therefore, unity is the driver.

If we could just remember that there is one body of Christ, one Holy Spirit, one hope, "one Lord, one faith, one baptism, one God and Father of all," we would stop trying to find ways to separate ourselves.

What do I mean by that? Everybody wants to be distinguished from everyone else. "I want to show you why I'm unique." "I want to show you why I'm different." But Paul is saying here, "No, you are one. You've been given different ministries, but you're united in one body. Focus on the one, and unity will follow."

The Body Consists of Many Members

This concept may sound familiar: everybody is different, yet we are one. You probably remember this from Paul's first letter to the Corinthians, chapter 12, verses 14-20:

> "**For the body is not one member, but many**. If the foot says, 'Because I am not a hand, I am not a part of the body,' it is not for this reason any less a part of the body. And if the ear says, 'Because I am not an eye, I am not a part of the body,' it is not for this reason any less a part of the body. If the whole body were an eye, where would the hearing be? If the whole were hearing, where would the sense of smell be? But now God has placed the members, each one of them, in the body, just as He desired. If they were all one member, where would the body be? **But now there are many members, but one body.**"

Here's the linchpin for the entire conversation: "many members, but one body." There are many different gifts, many different expressions of ministries, but one body. The eye cannot say to the hand, "I don't need you." The head cannot say to the feet, "I don't need you." What is Paul saying? "Even though you've been given a distinct ministry, you are still part of one body, serving one Lord, with one faith." We have to operate as one.

If you don't think the Scripture Paul is talking about there refers to the ministries, and you think, "Oh no, that's about spiritual gifts, not ministry," keep reading. When you get down to verses 27-31, he says,

> **"Now you are Christ's body, and individually members of it.** And God has appointed in the church, first apostles, second prophets, third teachers [there are the ministries again], then miracles, then gifts of healings, helps, administrations, various kinds of tongues. All are not apostles, are they? All are not prophets, are they? All are not teachers, are they? All are not workers of miracles, are they? All do not have gifts of healings, do they? All do not speak with tongues, do they? All do not interpret, do they? But earnestly desire the greater gifts."

Now, two things just came up in that set of Scriptures. One, we had confirmation that the conversation about being one body made up of many parts is applicable to the fivefold ministry. He talked about apostles, prophets, and teachers. That's one. But, he also introduced spiritual gifts. I've had some questions over the last few weeks about how spiritual gifts play into ministries. I will address that in the next chapter.

Different Capacities

Verse seven of Ephesians, chapter four, continues,

> "But to each one of us grace was given **according to the measure of Christ's gift.**"

What does that mean? "Grace," in this context, refers to a capacity—a volume question—we're given a capacity and an ability according to the grace that God wants to show us. So, when we read that sentence, "But to each one of us grace was given according to the measure of Christ's gift," it's saying that each one of us gets a different capacity and ability based on the measure of the gift that Christ gave us.

We've just opened up a whole new perspective: Some of us will operate in different capacities within the same ministry. For example, some may be more pastoral than others. There are people in my life whom I would describe as being 150% pastoral. Everything they think about revolves around the pastoral side of things. But then, there are people who do pastoral things, such as care for individuals, meet needs one-on-one and mentor others in a pastoral way, but their capacity may be different.

We've seen this concept multiple times in the New Testament. Let me show you from the Gospel of Luke, chapter 12, verse 48. Jesus says,

> "*From everyone who has been given much, much will be required; and to whom they entrusted much, of him they will ask all the more.*"

Jesus also tells the parable of the talents, as recorded in the Gospel of Matthew, chapter 25, verses 14-29. When the master comes back to see what the servants did with the talents they were given, each one is commended or reprimanded based on how he handled them, regardless of how many he was given. Jesus concludes the teaching by saying,

> *"For to everyone who has, more will be given, and he will have an abundance; but from the one who does not have, even what he does have shall be taken away."*

What do those two Scriptures mean in light of Ephesians, chapter four? There's an accountability for the measure of ministry that we've been given. There's an accountability you have for your particular capacity in that ministry.

Working Together

Now, let me recap these concepts for you: We are one body, God is over all and each one of us is given a "measure of Christ's gift." Why? It is so that we can operate in unity. The one God, who is over all, gave each of us a ministry so that we could work together, peaceably, in interdependence, as one body, even though each of us has been given something different.

What can I learn about working with other people in ministry because of "the measure of Christ's gift"? If someone is very strongly prophetic, they may seem harsh, always black-and-white about everything, maybe even bordering on rude or judgemental. They may not necessarily *be* judgemental, but they're so strongly prophetic, they see things more directly as right or wrong than others do.

A person who is very strongly apostolic is often considered not to be a "people person." In reality, that strongly-apostolic person is focused on managing the larger picture—how to lead the whole group in a certain direction, not just focusing on individuals. They're thinking about the masses.

Pastors are often thought of as disorganized, but maybe they just think that the time spent on individuals is more important than focusing on overall productivity. (That's spoken like an apostle, isn't it?) What I mean is, a pastor might say, "I'm not worried about the system, I'm worried about Sally, who's hurting and needs help..." They care for others individually. It's not that they're disorganized; it's that they're focused on people.

Highly evangelistic people might not like organized church, because they think everyone should be out sharing the gospel at Wawa or Walmart. But, maybe that's because they've been given a large measure of the evangelistic gift, so they focus on bringing the lost to Christ. Since we will be held accountable, however, we need to consider the capacity of the ministry God has given us.

Identifying and Preparing

I can imagine some of you are thinking, "Last week, I thought I was 110% prophetic. This week, I want to change that. I want to lower that bar just a little bit. Maybe I've just got a small measure of the prophetic—just enough to give a word to my spouse now and then." Or, "I thought I was apostolic last week, but what I meant was, I am just apostolic enough to tell people at the church how they should be doing things..." Or, "I'm a little evangelistic, but not *super*-evangelistic—not 'go to Wawa every weekend' evangelistic. Maybe once a quarter, after church, in the parking lot, I'll be an evangelist..."

I, myself, have been designed from the beginning as an "apostolic teacher." But I didn't start operating in an apostolic teaching ministry until I was 40 years old. Why not? Because God had me in training and preparation in the secular world, learning about the apostolic ministry and learning how to teach. Did I teach in church? Yes. I taught Sunday school classes. But I wasn't fully engaged in ministry until I was in my forties.

In other words, there's always a preparation time and a season for your ministry. You don't have to worry that you might have let God down by not jumping right into the ministry He's called you to. We need to talk about two things: identifying your calling and your preparation time. Just because God may have given you the apostolic ministry does not mean you should be in charge today. Just because God may have given you the ministry of teaching doesn't mean you should be teaching today.

There is always a preparation time, even though that ministry is a gift from Christ. How do I know that? Because if it weren't true, we would all be taught by 10-year-olds. Now, there are some 10-year-olds who can teach, no doubt, but the vast majority of us need to learn how to teach.

The Shepherd Boy Becomes King

Let me give you an example: David was anointed as king when he was a shepherd boy. David was anointed to be king, but he didn't go straight to Jerusalem and take over the throne. Why was David anointed as a shepherd boy in the field, but only became king 17 years later? He was given a 17-year preparation plan so that he could learn to fight the lion and the bear. David had to learn what it was like to serve under a bad, jealous king so that he wouldn't become one himself. He had to be trained in military battle so that he could defend the nation of Israel as its king.[40]

Is This Your Season?

So, we need to remember there's always a preparation time in ministry. Bear in mind also, there will always be a season for your ministry.

We can look at people we know—maybe some of you are familiar with individuals like Billy Graham, who had a lifetime season of ministry. Our friend, Charles Carrin, has been in ministry for 74 years. But, not everyone has a lifetime season of ministry. Yours may start today or your ministry may not begin for five years. When I was called into ministry, it was three years before I stepped into it. It may be that the season of your ministry is already done, and it's time for you to rest and to mentor others.

Where do I get this idea about seasons? Even Jesus didn't start His Messianic ministry until He was 30 years old, and then He had a three-year ministry. Then, His season was over. The season of His ministry was just a little over three years.

If you're concerned or anxious over whether you're being used correctly right now, maybe you are simply trying to please God, instead of waiting for God to open the door He's designed for you to walk through.

God isn't going to give up on you, so you can chill out. You're not being disobedient to God or neglectful of His call, unless

---

[40] 1 Samuel 16-17; 2 Samuel 2, 5, 8

you *know* what you're supposed to be doing and are resisting it. If that's the case, enjoy the belly of the whale.

God isn't in a hurry. You are going to fulfill the ministry He designed for you. You may choke on a bunch of seaweed and saltwater, but you're going to do it. No need to hit the panic button.

God knew, here and now, in Stuart, Florida, in 2024, in August and September, that you were going to be exposed to the fivefold ministry concept. Maybe you recognized something about yourself, and you didn't know it was a ministry. Maybe you didn't understand it was part of God's design, but now you do, and this is part of God's preparation for you to begin using the ministry He's called you into.

In the final chapter, we'll talk about how spiritual gifts interplay with the fivefold ministry. I'll explain why some people operate in more than one ministry and how God is able to use multiple ministries in some people's lives.

If this message is stirring something in you and you're thinking, "I get it; I'm ready to go," please find a trusted friend to pray with you. Ask them to pray to identify that ministry that God has given you. Pray about your preparation time and how to approach your calling.

Father God, we are Yours. We are dedicated to You, submitted to You, ready to be called into ministry — called into battle — called into pastoring, called into the apostolic, called into the prophetic, called into the evangelistic, called into teaching, based on Your design. Make it clear to us, press upon us with dreams and visions and confirmations, and seal it in us so we can go through our preparation time and be released into bringing Your Kingdom

FIVEFOLD FRAMEWORK

together as one.
In Jesus' name, Amen.

RESURRECTING UNITY

FIVEFOLD FRAMEWORK

RESURRECTING GIFTS

This book has addressed the "fivefold ministry" that's described in the Book of Ephesians, chapter four. We've talked about variations of each of the five ministries and about common pitfalls in each ministry. In this chapter, we're going to expand our study, because I believe there are two areas we need to cover before we close out the series.[41]

One question to be considered is, What about operating in multiple ministries? Can a person operate in more than one ministry? Another question is, How do spiritual gifts and the fivefold ministry work together? We'll try to answer those two questions in this chapter.

We'll begin with our base Scripture, from Paul's letter to the church in Ephesus, chapter four, verses 11-13. The Apostle Paul is writing to the Ephesians about the structure of the church, which is the physical representation of Christ on earth, and about the purpose God has for designing His church in this way.

> **"And He gave some as apostles, and some as prophets, and some as evangelists, and some as pastors and teachers**, for the equipping of the saints for the work of service, to the

---

[41] Based on the message, "Resurrecting Gifts," September 15, 2024. https://reviveusnow.com/watch

building up of the body of Christ; until we all attain to the unity of the faith and of the knowledge of the Son of God, to a mature man, to the measure of the stature which belongs to the fullness of Christ."

Multiple Ministries?

Can believers operate in multiple ministries when it comes to the fivefold ministry? I believe they can. Scripture actually gives us examples of people who were working in more than one ministry.

For example, the Apostle Peter was, obviously, apostolic; yet, Jesus gave him instructions to "feed My sheep," as a pastor would.[42] Peter operated in the apostolic and in the pastoral ministries.

If you look at the Apostle John, who wrote the Gospel of John and several letters to the believers, (1 John, 2 John and 3 John), the language he used is very loving, very people centric. He refers to his followers as his "little children." Perhaps John is a pastor who also operated as an apostle.

Reading the Book of James, it's hard to recognize whether James is a teacher or if he's functioning as a prophet. He's definitely teaching and explaining doctrine, but he's speaking in such black-and-white terms that you wonder, "Is this guy on the prophetic side of things?" Maybe James operated in both ministries.

If you look at the ministry of a guy named Stephen, in the Book of the Acts of the Apostles, we see that he was chosen

---

[42] John 21:15-17

to head up a feeding program in the very first church in Jerusalem. The widows of the Hellenistic Jews (Jews that were of Greek origin) were getting overlooked in the food distribution, apparently, and so Stephen was chosen as one of seven men to oversee that the widows were properly cared for. Does that mean he functioned as a pastor? It's also noted that Stephen worked in signs, wonders, and miracles,[43] which you would expect from an evangelist. Could it be that Stephen worked as an evangelist who was also overseeing a feeding program as an apostle would? We don't know, but that would mean he functioned in several ministries at once.

The young pastor, Timothy, oversaw the church congregation in Ephesus, and yet Paul tells him to "do the work of an evangelist."[44]

So, I believe Scripture does tell us that a person can operate in more than one of the ministries within the fivefold ministry.

Bringing Unity

But, let's not go overboard. Sometimes people see themselves operating in *every* ministry. They might be thinking, "Oh yeah, I'm like 30% prophetic and I'm 20% apostolic and I'm 20% evangelistic. I'm only 12% a teacher and yet 8% pastoral." We tend to have this thing where we want to view everything in our life based on those five ministries and making sure we're operating in each of them.

---

[43] Acts 6:8

[44] 2 Timothy 4:5

But, I believe, when you're doing that, you're totally destroying the fact that Christ gave to you one primary ministry. His purpose is to bring unity within the church, to build up His body. His design is to fulfill each of these ministries through all members of the church body working together.

I will say this, however: There is a ministry of the evangelist, and yet every one of us is supposed to share the gospel. There is a ministry of the teacher, and yet your coworker may say, "Can you explain this Scripture to me?" There is a ministry of the pastor, and yet, aren't we all supposed to love and care for one another? Yes, we are to "minister" to others as the Holy Spirit leads us in each situation. But, just because you're doing things in the other ministries does not mean that you've been given every ministry. Yes, we can work in all of them, but Christ gave you a ministry specific to you, so that you can work for the unity of the church. That's what the ministries do; they bring about unity.

I have said this before, I believe I am an "apostolic teacher," operating in both the apostolic and the teaching ministries. But, guess what? I still have to share the gospel like an evangelist. I still have to pastor and care about people. I still have to receive a prophetic word and deliver that to someone, as the Spirit leads.

Our original question was, "Can I operate in more than one ministry?" My answer is, yes. Yes, you can operate in more than one ministry. There are times and occasions, though, when it seems that the reason we are operating in more than one ministry is because there aren't enough people who have figured out what their ministry is, therefore, some of us have to double up.

FIVEFOLD FRAMEWORK

Everyone Plays a Part

There are plenty of people in the body of Christ, in the church. The question is, How many of them are operating in their primary ministry? I'm not asking that as condemnation at all. I'm hoping to bring conviction.

As we have been studying these five ministries, I'm hoping that you have realized, somewhere in this process, "I think God designed me to be a teacher, (or an evangelist, or a prophet), and as such, I need to figure out what my role in the body to bring about that unity is."

Unfortunately, in many churches today, in the United States and, probably, in South America, too, we've decided to leave all the ministry work to the senior pastor. He does it all! And so, we have built entire churches around a single figure. But that's not right. It's not right to have a single figure that does all of the ministries.

Now, make no mistake, anything with more than one head is a monster. But we don't have to worry about that, because that's not what Christ designed. When He designed the fivefold ministry, He said, "I need all of these operating in order to have unity. There may be an apostolic leader, there may be a prophetic leader, there may be a pastoral leader of that congregation, but all of those ministries should be operating."

So, part of why we're doing all of this is to say to you, "Maybe this is the season in your life that God is explaining to you, through this series, who you are and how you can contribute to the unity of the church body." Maybe He's awakening that in you right now.

Spiritual Gifts vs. Ministries

The second part of our conversation involves how the "spiritual gifts" relate to the fivefold ministry. I believe it's very common that the ministries and the giftings are confused. Why? It's confusing because both are called out as gifts to the church. You've been given the gift of grace in a ministry; you've been given a spiritual gift.

What happens is, when it comes to ministries, you're given a ministry by Christ and you're given a spiritual gift through the Holy Spirit. These are two separate operations. The fivefold ministry is separate from the spiritual gifts. So, let's take a look at the spiritual gifts. Following that, we'll go back and see how they relate to the ministries.

I want to talk about the spiritual gifts as they are listed in Paul's first letter to the Corinthians, chapter 12, beginning with verse four, and also in his letter to the Romans, chapter 12.

Before we read the First Corinthians passage, however, I'll remind you that every word in Scripture is there for a reason. Don't be casual in looking at the words. Think about every word and ask yourself why it was chosen.

Paul starts this conversation by identifying gifts and ministries. He says,

> "**Now there are varieties of gifts**, but the same Spirit. **And there are varieties of ministries**, and the same Lord. There are varieties of effects, but the same God who works all things in all persons."

That word, "effects" means "operations" in the Greek. God is empowering the operations of the church through giftings and ministries. Just so you can get that clearly, the Holy Spirit is going to give gifts; Christ is going to give ministries; but, God is going to work it all together.

Now, if you're going to study the spiritual gifts in First Corinthians, chapter 12, and you're going to ignore verse seven, don't study the spiritual gifts. If you don't get verse seven, then the rest of the passage is not going to have any value. In verse seven Paul, referring to the spiritual gifts, says,

> "But to each one is given the manifestation [the gift] of the Spirit **for the common good**."

You are not given spiritual gifts for your own benefit. You're not given spiritual gifts so that you can use them, so that you can display them, so that you can be proud of yourself. You're given spiritual gifts because we need them in the church. The church needs that spiritual gift and it has been given to you for the common good of the body.

Spiritual Gifts

Paul goes on to list the spiritual gifts, beginning with verse eight:

> "For to one is given the word of wisdom through the Spirit, [capital "S," referring to the Holy Spirit] and to another the word of knowledge according to the same Spirit; to another faith by the same Spirit, and to another gifts of healing by the one Spirit, and to another, the effecting of miracles, and to another prophecy, and to another the distinguishing of spirits, to another various kinds of tongues and to another the interpretation of tongues. But one and the same Spirit [Holy Spirit] works all

these things, distributing to each one individually just as He wills."

Oneness in the Body

So there we started our list of spiritual gifts. In verses 12-25, Paul goes into the discussion of the oneness in the body that believers enjoy. We studied this in the previous chapter, but for review, Paul begins by saying,

> **"For even as the body is one and yet has many members, and all the members of the body, though they are many, are one body, so also is Christ.** For by one Spirit we were all baptized into one body, whether Jews or Greeks, whether slaves or free, and we were all made to drink of one Spirit.
>
> "For the body is not one member, but many. If the foot says, "Because I am not a hand, I am not a part of the body," it is not for this reason any the less a part of the body. And if the ear says, "Because I am not an eye, I am not a part of the body," it is not for this reason any the less a part of the body. If the whole body were an eye, where would the hearing be? If the whole were hearing, where would the sense of smell be? But now God has placed the members, each one of them, in the body, just as He desired. If they were all one member, where would the body be? But now there are many members, but one body. And the eye cannot say to the hand, "I have no need of you"; or again the head to the feet, "I have no need of you." On the contrary, it

is much truer that the members of the body which seem to be weaker are necessary; and those members of the body which we deem less honorable, on these we bestow more abundant honor, and our less presentable members become much more presentable, whereas our more presentable members have no need of it. But God has so composed the body, giving more abundant honor to that member which lacked, so that there may be no division in the body, but that the members may have the same care for one another. And if one member suffers, all the members suffer with it; if one member is honored, all the members rejoice with it."

In this context — in the context of oneness in the body — Paul starts mentioning ministries and gifts together. Verses 27-28 say,

"Now you are Christ's body, and individually members of it. **And God has appointed in the church, first apostles, second prophets, third teachers, then miracles, then gifts of healings, helps, administrations, various kinds of tongues.** All are not apostles, are they? All are not prophets, are they? All are not teachers, are they? All are not workers of miracles, are they? All do not have gifts of healings, do they? All do not speak with tongues, do they? All do not interpret, do they? But earnestly desire the greater gifts."

So, what is Paul saying? He's saying that God is affecting all of these operations — spiritual gifts and ministries — in the body, because of our oneness in Christ.

We Are One Body in Christ

Now we're going to read a portion of Paul's letter to the Romans, because Paul included similar teachings to that group of believers in chapter 12, verses one through eight.

> "Therefore I urge you, brethren, by the mercies of God, to present your bodies a living and holy sacrifice, acceptable to God which is your spiritual service of worship. And do not be conformed to this world, but be transformed by the renewing of your mind, so that you may prove what the will of God is, that which is good and acceptable and perfect.
>
> For through the grace given to me I say to everyone among you not to think more highly of himself than he ought to think; but to think so as to have sound judgment, as God has allotted to each a measure of faith. **For just as we have many members in one body and all the members do not have the same function, so we, who are many, are one body in Christ, and individually members one of another."**

Paul says, "You've got to present yourself as a living sacrifice. You have got to renew your mind. And, by the way, don't think too highly of yourself, because we're all members of one body." Now, he's going to identify part of the ways we are one body, as he continues in verse six,

> "Since we have gifts that differ according to the grace given to us, each of us is to exercise

them accordingly: if prophecy, according to the proportion of his faith; if service, in his serving; or he who teaches, in his teaching; or he who exhorts, in his exhortation; he who gives, with liberality; he who leads, with diligence; he who shows mercy, with cheerfulness."

We see that the conversation here is about all of these things, spiritual gifts and ministries, operating in the church.

This happens to be one of those places where people get giftings and ministries confused. I think that's a legitimate confusion if you don't stay in the context of what Paul is saying. But, within this context, he's not teaching on gifts and ministries separately; he's teaching on offering whatever you have been given—the "grace-gift" given to you—and using that gift or ministry sacrificially, as a spiritual service to God.

Highlighting the Gifts

Paul did, however, bring up some new gifts that weren't listed in chapter 12 of First Corinthians. I would like to combine the two lists and basically explain what each gift is, so that later, when I connect that gift to the ministries, you can see how those two things work together.

If you want to go deeper into any of these gifts, I've taught on each individual one, in detail, in the past. You can go to our Revive Church YouTube channel[45] to find a message on the different gifts, if you want to do that. In this chapter, however, I'm not going to dive deeply into each gift, but I'll highlight the key points.

---

[45] https://www.youtube.com/@Reviveusnow

We'll start with the ones we just read from First Corinthians, chapter 12, combined with those in Romans, chapter 12.

- The first gift mentioned is the "word of wisdom." (1 Corinthians 12:8)

What is a "word of wisdom"? Is that something you heard your smart grandfather say? No, it's not about having wisdom in the generic, worldly sense. It is wisdom that is specific to a moment, an indisputable explanation or uncanny information that's given. Maybe in today's words, the easiest way to identify a word of wisdom is to call it a "drop the mic" moment. You just laid a bomb out there and nobody can refute it; it cleared everything up; it made so much sense. "Wow, what a word!" It was a word of "wisdom." Often, those words of wisdom create an action.

- Secondly, there is the "word of knowledge." (1 Corinthians 12:8)

This is the supernatural ability to know something that you could not have known from a natural standpoint. For example, imagine you're in a grocery store, and you hear the Holy Spirit say to you, "Go and ask that lady about her son." You have no idea who she is, or what's going on with her son, but you obey the prompting. You walk up to the woman and ask her, "Hey, is something going on with your son?" And she breaks down in tears. You just received a word of knowledge — something you didn't get naturally, something you didn't know about — and it was a setup that God used to reveal Himself to that person. It was a "word of knowledge."

Sometimes, during a service, someone will receive a word of knowledge and will speak it out. "There's someone here with

FIVEFOLD FRAMEWORK

pain in their back..." Or, "Someone has a numbness in the side of their face." That's a word of knowledge, given through that speaker, to the body, so that we can pray for your healing.

- Next, "faith" is mentioned as a gift.
  (1 Corinthians 12:9)

In this context, we're not talking about faith as the salvation tool, where you study Scripture and you build up your faith. We're talking about a "gift of faith." It's a supernatural endowment of faith for a particular plan of God. It's given as a gift; it's not something you build up.

It is a divinely-given boost of faith—that moment when someone, in the middle of something we're going through, says, "No, we need to stand on the Word of God here. We need to move forward. We need to do this thing that He's calling us to do." The result of that one person's "gift of faith" is that everyone else gets motivated. There was a word of faith released so that we can put our trust in God for that particular thing.

- Next, there are "gifts of healing."
  (1 Corinthians 12:9)

This is the supernatural ability to pray and ask for healing to be demonstrated in others, and that healing is accomplished. That's an actual gift. There are some people given the gift of healing. I pray for people to get healed; sometimes they get healed, sometimes they don't. When they don't, I find somebody with the gift of healing and ask, "Could you pray for them? because you have the gift of healing and we want that person to be healed."

- Then, there is the "effecting of miracles."
  (1 Corinthians 12:10)

There is an actual gift for the "effecting of miracles," which is the empowerment to use the power of God to affect something in a way that cannot be accomplished in the natural. It's a broad category. It's saying that there's a power that exists in God, and some people are gifted with the ability to call on that power, in order to affect something in the natural. It could be to get somebody to change their mind; it could be to remove a "mountain," an incredible difficulty in someone's life; it could be the calling forth of a provision that is needed. Those are the "effecting of miracles."

- Next, the gift of "prophecy."
  (1 Corinthians 12:10)

This is not talking about the ministry of the prophetic, as in, the one within the fivefold ministry. Paul is talking about the gift of prophecy. In the ministry of the prophetic, that's someone who has been given the ministry of hearing from God and delivering that message to the leaders of the church.

The "gift of prophecy," in very simple terms, is when the Holy Spirit gives you words to deliver to someone. Now, maybe you've had this: "You know, I don't work in the prophetic ministry. I don't feel like I have that kind of connection and working with God, to speak into the leaders of the church or speaking to the church, as a whole. But man, the other day, God told me to go over to this friend of mine and just say, 'That bill you can't pay? It's going to be taken care of for you.' And, all of a sudden, I've got a word..."

That's a "prophetic word." That's the gift of prophecy operating in the moment. You don't have to be in the prophetic ministry to operate in the gift of prophecy.

- The next gift listed is the "distinguishing of spirits." (1 Corinthians 12:10)

This is not the same as "discernment." Some versions of the Bible have translated that incorrectly as a "gift of discernment," but discernment is learned. The Scriptures are very clear that we learn discernment.

But, this refers to the "gift of distinguishing spirits." It's the ability to determine whether evil spirits or spirits of God are present and at work in a situation. It's the ability to recognize, "That illness, that's a demonic oppression. That's not a cold because you were outside last night; that's demonic." In the same way, "Man, there's an angelic host that joined our worship today. Did you see that? Did you feel that?" A person with the gift of distinguishing spirits has that type of supernatural assessment of the situation.

- "Various kinds of tongues" and the "interpretation of tongues" are listed together. (1 Corinthians 12:10)

I did four sermons in a row on tongues. If you want to learn about tongues, I refer you to those four messages. "Tongues" are spiritual languages that declare the glories of God. Therefore, the "interpretation of tongues" is the endowment, or the ability, to interpret those spiritual languages that get spoken.

- Next, "service" (Romans 12:7) and "helps" (1 Corinthians 12:27).

These are gifts you don't even know, that you recognize in people, but after this, you will. The gifts of service and helps encompass the desire to be hospitable or to serve others.

Do you have that friend that you can call that always says "Yes"?

"Hey, I need something."
"Okay, what do you need?"
"I need you to pick me up."
"Okay, what time do you need me to be there?" ...

There is a spiritual gift of service and helps. My oldest daughter has that gift. You call her, you ask her to do anything, and she says, "Okay, okay, I'll get that done." It's a fulfilling thing for her, because it's a spiritual gift.

- The next one we'll talk about is the gift of "exhortation." (Romans 12:8)

This is the ability to build others up and encourage them. This is that person you call whenever you're struggling. For me, it was a man named Brad Sutton, a very good friend of mine. As a matter of fact, one of my entries into worship ministry was through Brad Sutton.

Over the 17 or 18 years that we knew each other, if I was ever down, if I was ever confused, I called Brad. Why? Because Brad just seemed to find a way - in 20 minutes - to make me feel like the world was amazing and everything was great, that all my troubles were going to be absolutely fine. He had the gift of exhortation or encouragement. He could build you up in a moment. There are people that have that gift.

- The gift of "giving" is the supernatural desire to provide for the Kingdom financially. (Romans 12:8)

How do I know when a person has the gift of giving? They think differently than everybody else does. Everybody else thinks, "Okay, I need to make sure I give something to the Lord...Maybe I'm a tither. Maybe I'm a giver. Maybe when big projects come along, I need to sacrifice and give..."

A person with the gift of giving actually thinks this way: "How much do I need to survive so that I can send the rest into the Kingdom?" "How much do I need in order for me to make my rent, pay my bills, meet all of my responsibilities so that I can send more into the Kingdom?"

- The gift of "leadership" is the supernatural ability to direct a group of people to a common goal. (Romans 12:8)

We know this: Whether it's at your work or in your circle of friends, whenever it comes down to needing something to get done, we always pick this person to be in charge.
"Can you make that happen?"
"Yeah, I'll make that happen."

- The gift of "administrations" is the ability to organize and manage resources.
(1 Corinthians 12:28)

A lot of people will confuse the gift of administration with the apostolic ministry, but they are different things. The apostolic ministry is about organization, structure, building, empowerment, setting things in place. The gift of administration is about making a list and "checking it twice." It's about knowing that things are put in order. It's about having an Excel spreadsheet and knowing that you've got a follow-up plan. It's a different gifting than the apostolic ministry.

- Finally, there's the gift of "mercy."
  (Romans 12:8)

Mercy is the legitimate ability to show empathy and compassion. We see that most often as a gift when somebody is showing empathy and compassion towards someone that he didn't even know was hurting. They sense the needs of others because of their gifting. They see hurts and pains that other people don't necessarily see. They go minister to people based on the direction they're given with that gift. That's the gift of "mercy."

The Holy Spirit Works All These Things

I believe that these gifts are given to the body and that every Holy Spirit-filled believer can operate in any of these capacities.

I used to think that you were just given one of these giftings, because the Scripture says, "...to each one is given a manifestation of the Spirit..." I thought you got one and that was it. You were kind of "stuck" with that one. You may not like it, but that's your gifting.

Then I started really meditating on First Corinthians, chapter 12, verse 11. I want you to consider this Scripture:

> "But one and the same Spirit [the Holy Spirit] works all these things, **distributing to each one individually just as He wills**."

The gifts are distributed to each person just as the Holy Spirit wills. There is something that captivates me about that statement: If the gifts are distributed according to God's will, who am I to argue with what He gives to somebody else? Who am I to argue with to whom He gives it; how much He gives it; when He gives it; or, why He gives it to him?

God, through the Holy Spirit, is going to distribute the gifts however He wants to. He does what He wants to do when it comes to distributing the gifts. I love that, "just as He wills," —just whatever He wants to do theologically. The Holy Spirit does whatever God wants. I'm not going to question what God wants to do as far as to whom He gives what gift, when, how and how much.

Pursue Love

Now, let me couple that thought with chapter 14 of First Corinthians, verse one. This is where the focus pushes into multiple giftings.

Paul has just had a conversation, in chapter 13, where he said, "The greatest things that we can have are faith, hope and love. But, what you *really* want is love. 'The greatest of these is love.'[46] If you have love, then you're on the right track."

He begins verse one, therefore, saying,

> "Pursue love…"

---

[46] 1 Corinthians 13:13

He's saying, "Press into love; know love,..." Then he says,

> "...yet **desire earnestly spiritual gifts**,..."

"I want you to *intentionally* want spiritual gifts." Now, it does say "gifts" in the plural. We could apply that to an individual and say, "He's saying that he wants us to individually desire spiritual gifts." Or, we could interpret that to mean that he's telling the church, "I want you, as a church, to desire the spiritual gifts."

But he goes on,

> "...but especially that you may prophesy."

So, "Desire the spiritual gifts..." but combine that with, ..."especially that you may prophesy."

Paul is likely saying, "I want you to desire tongues, but especially that you would prophesy." "I want you to desire words of knowledge, but especially that you would prophesy." How can you desire both and then desire one more than the other?

How could he tell you to want this one thing, but want this other thing even more? It would be like me telling you to desire eggs for breakfast. "I would like everybody to have eggs for breakfast. I want you to earnestly go and order eggs for breakfast, but *really* order steak."

Sounds funny, doesn't it? "I'm good with you wanting eggs, but you should really want steak..." So, am I saying that you can't have the eggs? Or, am I saying, "Get the eggs, but get the steak, if you can"? Yeah, I think that's what he's saying here.

Paul is saying, "Desire all the gifts, but have the greatest desire for the gift of prophecy." Why? Why would he be telling us there's one gift that needs to grab our attention the most; that our greatest desire should be for prophesying? Let's continue reading verses two through five:

> "For one who speaks in a tongue does not speak to men but to God; for no one understands, but in his spirit he speaks mysteries. **But one who prophesies speaks to men for edification and exhortation and consolation.** One who speaks in a tongue edifies himself; but one who prophesies edifies the church. Now I wish that you all spoke in tongues, but even more that you would prophesy; and greater is one who prophesies than one who speaks in tongues, unless he interprets, so that the church may receive edifying.

Here, Paul is telling us that prophesying is the act of edifying, exhorting and consoling one another. He says, "The most important thing I want you to go after is building each other up, speaking life into each other, encouraging each other, edifying each other."

If Paul meant to instruct us that we would only have one gift, why wouldn't the Holy Spirit say, based on First Corinthians, chapter 14, verse one, "Since I want you mostly to prophesy, that's the only gift I will give you; that's the one I want you to have most"? Why didn't God just give everybody the gift of prophecy? No, He said, "I want you all to want that, but I also want you to want the other gifts."

Gifts and Ministries Working Together

So, we have these gifts that we're supposed to pursue and desire, and we have this fivefold ministry framework within which we work. How do these things work together?

I believe each one of us is a Father God-designed puzzle, with different pieces that create the picture that is you. It comes all together in a beautiful picture, but each one of you has a different puzzle piece and a different picture. Yet, God has designed each one of your puzzles individually.

Because of the design that you have, you are created to do certain things in the church, which is Christ's body. Have you ever had a problem in your life, in your friendships, in your work, whatever it is, and you find yourself saying, "I know exactly who should handle this; so-and-so is perfect to take care of this…"? When you make that kind of statement, what's actually going on there is, you're identifying the person who has the right ministry and gifting combination for whatever the issue before you is.

There are things that some of you are right to handle that I'm not the best person to handle at all. Why? Because your "puzzle," your mixture of ministries and gifts, is different from mine. Some situations need you or you or you, not me, to handle them.

Let's explore what it looks like to operate in one of the ministries along with spiritual gifts. How do they work together? I'm going to start with some simple examples to begin giving you demonstrations of how these things work together.

FIVEFOLD FRAMEWORK

- What if we have a person who is strongly pastoral, who has also been given the gift of administration?

This person loves people: He wants to be around people; he wants to help people; it just fills him with joy to be with other people. But, because of the gift of administration, these are the things you'll see: He will spend his time caring for people, but he will have a follow-up system to make sure to check on them again. He will even put something in his calendar to remind him that he needs to call so-and-so, to make sure he's okay, on a certain date.

He will keep a list of what the person said the last time they talked, so that he can look it over before going back to talk to them again. "I don't want to miss anything that they care about. I want to remember what they said."

He will have an inventory of things, like books and helpful people and phone numbers, that he keeps in order to pass on to other people. He cares so much about other people, but that gift of administration says, "I have got to do it in an organized fashion."

- What if you have an evangelist who delights to go evangelizing anywhere, at any time, in order to share the gospel with someone; but, who also operates in the gift of prophecy?

How do we see that the evangelist works in the gift of prophecy? Here's how: When she goes to Walmart, she says, "Give me just a minute. I think I'm supposed to go and talk to that person, but I want God to tell me what it is I'm supposed to say to get the door open." Then she hears the Holy Spirit prompting her to approach the woman with, "Tell me about your daughter."

She's looking for a prophetic word to open the door for evangelism. She has the gift of prophecy, so she's guided by that gift to use that within her primary ministry.

- What do you do if you have a teacher who loves the Word of God, loves digging in and getting revelation from the Word, who also has the gift of mercy?

What does that look like? Maybe you can tell, because he frequently wants to teach on the compassion of Christ. He wants to ensure that people are led to Scriptures that will help them when they're in need. He will teach about the ways that Jesus reached hurting people. He will love to teach on the woman caught in adultery.[47] Why? So he can point out the mercy that Christ showed to this individual. That's the teaching ministry, combined with a gift of mercy.

- What happens if an apostolic person has the gift of distinguishing spirits?

Apostolic: organizing, set it up, make sure it's covered, make sure the masses are discipled. How does that work if you are working in the gift of distinguishing spirits? The apostle will ensure that there are qualified, knowledgeable people available when someone is dealing with a demonic oppression. "I see this demonic oppression on you; I happen to have these people over here, who are trained in that; I'm going to bring them to you, so they can help you with that."

He will make sure that there are deliverance classes available so that the church can understand spiritual warfare. He will

---

[47] John 8:1-11

want you to know that there is a battle going on in the spiritual realm, so that you'll be able to recognize demonic activity, when it's at work in your life. He will want you to be able to see it.

Not only the demonic, but he will also be consistent to point out when an angelic host is working in your territory. The apostolic person with the distinguishing of spirits is looking to ensure that everybody understands that spiritual realm.

- What if there is a highly prophetic person and her gift is exhortation?

Her gift is edifying others, building people up, and yet, she's a highly prophetic person. This is what I call one of the "nice prophets."

There are all kinds of prophets. Some prophets always seem to deliver a call to repentance and holiness: "The church is in trouble…" and "The church is falling…" and so on and so on.

Then there are prophets who say, "There are some great things coming! The Lord has plans for us. He's going to get us through this! There's a shift coming; there's an elevation coming; there's something new in the spiritual realm on its way…" These types of prophets are working in exhortation. They're working at building up the church body through the prophetic messages they're hearing from the Lord. They focus on those type of things.

Completing the Puzzle

We see, therefore, that the ministry and the gift go together. This helps us to understand another person's design better. When we are able to see the difference between the ministry and the spiritual gift, and how they work together, we have a clearer picture of the "puzzle" God designed us to be.

A person with the gift of prophecy is not necessarily working in the prophetic ministry. A person with a gift of administration is not necessarily apostolic. A person who works in the gift of mercy isn't always strictly pastoral. A person that works with the gift of words of wisdom is not necessarily operating in the ministry of the teacher.

So, how do you tell the difference between a ministry and the spiritual gift? I believe that ministries are larger in a person's life than giftings. Your ministry would be considered the baseline role you have in the Kingdom. It would be the foundation from which the gifts are demonstrated. You're operating in this ministry *and* you have these gifts.

Why do I take that view? First of all, there are only five ministries; and, secondly, there are all these gifts. Remember that the ministries are for the unity of the church. Spiritual gifts are for the common good of the church. How in the world can there be a common good, if there's no unity? There has to be unity, so that there is something in common, that we can work toward, that would be "for the common good."

The fivefold ministry brings unity to the body. When we have unity in the body, we can begin operating in the gifts, because the gifts are for the common good of the body. If the body is not in unity — if it's not together — what's the purpose of a "common-good" gift? I think what we do is, we look for the baseline of the ministry and then we watch how gifts are used. Both the ministry and the spiritual gifts are critical. Both are essential.

Identifying and Activating

Now, if a person is operating in multiple ministries and then you put two or three giftings in there, it can get really complex and complicated. But, I believe we struggle with that in the church because not enough of us understand and are operating in our ministry and our spiritual gifts.

I'm asking you, therefore, to evaluate yourself and determine which of the fivefold ministry categories you feel you fall into. The next step, then, would be to have a conversation with someone who operates in that ministry. You can ask them some questions to possibly confirm what you're sensing.

- "I think this way - is that in line with how you think?"
- "I do these things - is that in line with what you do?"
- "Is there any advice you could give me?"
- "How did you get started in this ministry?"

Beginning now, we're intending for you to identify and start activating your given ministry. We're saying, if one aspect of the fivefold ministry describes you, we want to start talking to you about it. We want to start talking to you about operating in that pastoral ministry that you've been given. We want to start talking about getting you into our prophetic group. We want to start talking to you about going out and evangelizing, or at least assisting in evangelizing.

Father God, in the name of Jesus, we declare that You have a plan and purpose for this study that we've done. You are opening up Your church body to operate as it was designed to operate, to engage Your people in bringing a unity and a common good in this house. We honor that. We honor Your system. We honor Your designs. God, we want to step out boldly in faith; we want to understand our ministry more; we want to engage in that ministry more; we want to be connected to that ministry at the church.

Father God, as we come before You with our various needs, through the power of Your spirit, break any bondages. Bust down those walls. Remove the diagnoses for Your glory, for Your honor, for Your praise.
In Jesus' name, Amen.

ABOUT THE AUTHOR

Todd Mozingo, Senior Pastor, apostolic teacher, husband, father, and grandfather.

Raised in an ultra-conservative church atmosphere, to later being baptized in the Spirit, Todd has transitioned from one side of Christianity to the other. But the direction God gave him was to bring the two back together. The Word of God and the Spirit of God must be united in the body of Christ.

In 2000, the Holy Spirit spoke to Todd and told him to leave the secular world of manufacturing management and enter the King's service. His wife had cancer at the time and would pass on to her eternity only months after he received this word. But when the call came, he entered the King's service and got his Seminary degree. Progressing from one conservative, traditional church to another, and increasing in responsibility in each, he was eventually the Senior Pastor of a growing conservative church.

On a trip to Bogota, Columbia, to understand the revival happening there, the Holy Spirit radically baptized Todd with the baptism of the Holy Spirit. Rejected by his congregation, Todd started proclaiming the message of putting the Word of God and the Spirit of God back together with the birth of Revive Church in Stuart, FL. Through the challenges of combining the charismatic and the conservative groups, Revive Church has become a place where Bible-based miracles, Scriptural healings, Word-centered

ABOUT THE AUTHOR

deliverances, and salvations through the gospel of the kingdom of God are a normal part of their church services.

OTHER BOOKS BY TODD MOZINGO

<u>LOVE NEVER LIES</u> (2023)

We live in a society and culture that is not only getting comfortable with lies, but is now telling Christians that they need to accept those lies. And, too often, the Christian's response is either tolerance, agreement or deciding that Jesus would just be kind and not respond with the truth. But when we look in Scripture, we find a different Jesus. We find a Jesus who told the truth - *always.* This loving Savior knew how to speak the truth in love and we need to learn to do the same, because *love never lies.*

<u>OLD IS THE NEW: CONNECTING COVENANTS</u> (2022)

The Old Testament is filled with stories that seem amazing on their own, but they also leave questions. If they are history, and not a part of the New Covenant that we have with Christ today, then why do we need these stories at all? What are they there for? Could it be that those stories were recorded and saved for us because there is something they can teach us? Could it be that those stories actually help us understand God and the New Covenant He has made with us? Could it be that somehow those stories guide, teach and help us understand what God has for us as New Covenant believers? Could there be hidden mysteries in these stories that actually give us revelation for today?

OTHER BOOKS BY TODD MOZINGO

GOD VINDICATION (2022)

It is without a doubt the biggest topic on planet earth. To compare anything else to God is to say that there are other infinite topics in the universe to discuss. God is the only infinite, overwhelming, never-ending, constant revelation in existence. So, why write a book about God? Because there is so much to explore. The world wants to remove Him, the enemy wants to distort Him, believers want to exalt Him, and the unbeliever wants to ignore Him. But God is right, reasonable, and justified as the Creator, the Almighty, the powerful Father who loves you as an individual, deeply and completely. He is **God.**

JESUS VINDICATION (2022)

Who is Jesus? Just how human was He? How did He pray? Did He pray like you and I pray? He could heal people, but did He do it like you and I are supposed to, or was it different because He is Jesus? He cried, but did He cry like you and I cry? What was he doing during Old Testament times? Was He just waiting around to come to earth?

There are so many questions about Jesus' humanity versus His divinity. In *Jesus Vindication* we take a look at Jesus, the divine and the human.

HOLY SPIRIT VINDICATION (2022)

The Holy Spirit causes too much trouble in church today. He tends to make things get emotional and out of control, right? So, maybe the best thing to do is to shut Him down and make Him take a back seat. Because, after all, if it's not in the Bible, then it should not happen in a church service, right? Without the Holy Spirit's interference everything can be easily managed, easily controlled, and we can get out of church on time. Everyone seems to have the nice, simple, in-and-out church service that makes us comfortable. Why has the church decided that He is too complicated for people to understand? When something is right, reasonable, and justified, we will fight for it. Isn't the Holy Spirit a right, reasonable, and justified Presence? It's time for the church to fight for the presence of the Holy Spirit. It's time to vindicate the Holy Spirit.

GET IT TOGETHER: A GUIDE TO REVIVE YOUR MARRIAGE (2022)

Marriage can be one of the most difficult relationships in life! We come initially with excitement and great hope for the future. Then, life happens and the struggles begin. But if Christ is the bridegroom of His church, then how is this thing called marriage supposed to work? Did God set up a relationship called marriage that can actually be a long-lasting, loving relationship? *Get It Together* goes straight to the Word. We look directly and in depth at God's design for marriage to see if we can understand how it is supposed to work. Maybe, just maybe, the world has been teaching us a marriage plan that is destined to fail. But God has a plan that leads to a joy-filled, amazing relationship with our spouse!

NOT MY FRUIT: LET THE HOLY SPIRIT PRODUCE THE FRUIT (2022)

We all know that God wants us to be calm, warm, wonderful, loving people who act Christ-like in every situation. But, how's that working for you? We all struggle to be patient, faithful, and to exercise self-control. As a matter of fact, God gives us a list of nine things we are supposed to walk out, and it's never easy. But here's the problem: we can't do it on our own. After reading *Not My Fruit*, you will find out that you are not supposed to. Why not? Because it's not *your* fruit, it is the fruit of the Holy Spirit. Understanding how the Holy Spirit works will bring you great peace and satisfaction in your walk as a Christ-like believer. So, if you are looking for help with the fruit of the Spirit, look no further than the Holy Spirit.

MISSING PIECES: KINGDOM REVELATIONS (Revised 2023)

We are all missing pieces of the big picture of the Bible and the kingdom of God. We have accepted some things, but when asked, we really cannot explain them, because we just accepted them as information without understanding. But when someone puts a missing piece in place, the greater picture becomes easier to see and understand. The Bible calls this *revelation*. Scriptural revelation is when we begin to see the things "hidden *for* us," that we thought were "hidden *from* us." As this revelation grows, we get a greater and greater understanding of the massive amount of information that the Bible holds for us. Contained in this book are some of the major missing pieces that have been revealed to me. I hope that as you read, these missing pieces will help you on your journey to a greater revelation of what God has for you!

FIVEFOLD FRAMEWORK

FLIP THE SCRIPT: A FRESH LOOK AT SCRIPTURE (2021)

"Maybe I need to look at that Scripture again…"

What if, in our attempt to get something from Scripture, we are missing the point of that Scripture? What if, in our desire to do better and walk out Christianity more closely in line with Scripture, we are missing what the Scripture is actually trying to teach us? What if, in our zeal to get practical daily tips, we are missing Kingdom revelations? *Flip the Script* takes a fresh look at what the Scriptures are meant to teach us about the kingdom of God, so that application comes from spiritual understanding, instead of from behavioral modifications.

HIDE AND SEEK: LIES THAT HIDE IN OUR BELIEF SYSTEM (2018)

The enemy wants to hide lies in our belief system to keep us from all that God has for us. This book helps expose some of the common lies so that we can remove them. In this book, you will learn some of the most common lies we are told, that we are tempted to believe, and you will learn how to avoid providing hiding places for those lies and how to remove them from your belief system. Once you know how to play the game of "Hide and Seek" with the enemy, he will never again have a safe place to hide. You will be empowered to make future decisions based on the light of the truth of God, rather than on the hidden lies of satan.

BATTLE PLAN: YOUR GUIDE TO FIGHT AGAINST THE SPIRITUAL FORCES OF DARKNESS (Revised 2022)

What if we took 50 men and women, and we went out to the city and we began praying over people and handing out sandwiches and handing out T-shirts that said, "Can't we all get along?" Will we accomplish as much doing that than if we decided to go out and pray over our city and pray that the spiritual forces that are binding people would be removed from this area, so that the Spirit of God would be free to flow? Then we would be the front line. We're going to clear the way for the Holy Spirit to come in and do what the Holy Spirit wants. We are going to accomplish more because we've assessed the battle and listened to the Holy Spirit for His plan. This book highlights that plan from the Word of God and equips each follower of Jesus for the spiritual battle raging around us. That battle is happening, whether we want it to or not. The question is whether we will answer the call of God and engage through His power to defeat His enemies and ours.

All books are available on Amazon.

Made in the USA
Columbia, SC
01 November 2024